Anonymous

Buffalo Bill's wild West

And congress of rough riders of the world

Anonymous

Buffalo Bill's wild West
And congress of rough riders of the world

ISBN/EAN: 9783337728014

Printed in Europe, USA, Canada, Australia, Japan

Cover: Foto ©ninafisch / pixelio.de

More available books at **www.hansebooks.com**

WILD
WEST
COL. W. F. CODY.
AND
CONGRESS OF ROUGH RID
OF THE WORLD
HISTORICAL SKETCHES.

THE

STATE OF NEBRASKA

TO ALL TO WHOM THESE PRESENTS SHALL COME GREETING.

Know Ye, that I, John M. Thayer, Governor of the State of Nebraska, reposing special trust and confidence in the integrity, patriotism and abilities of Colonel William F. Cody on behalf and in the name of the State do hereby Appoint and Commission him Aid-de-Camp-in-Chief on the Staff of the Commander-in-Chief with the rank of Brigadier General and do authorize and empower him to discharge the duties of said office according to law.

In Testimony Whereof, I have hereunto subscribed my name and caused to be affixed the Great Seal of the State. Done at Lincoln this 23rd day of November AD 1889

John M. Thayer

By the Governor.

Ben R. Cowdery

Secretary of State

BUFFALO BILL'S WILD WEST

AND

CONGRESS OF ROUGH RIDERS OF THE WORLD

COL. W. F. CODY.

CHICAGO, ILL.—1893.

STAFF OF "BUFFALO BILL'S" WILD WEST COMPANY.

COL. W. F. CODY ("Buffalo Bill"), President. **NATE SALSBURY**, Vice-President and Manager.

JOHN M. BURKE - - - - - - - - - - - - - - General Manager

Albert E. Sheible - - Business Representative § L. J. Loring - - - - - - - Orator

Carter Couturier - - - - Advertising Agent § Lew Parker - - - - Contracting Agent

Iulé Keen - - - - - - - - Treasurer § William Langan - - - - - Supply Agent

WILD WEST SCENERY BY - - - - - - - **A. BENDER**

COL. W. F. CODY.

NATE SALSBURY.

BUFFALO BILL'S
WILD WEST

—AND—

CONGRESS OF ROUGH RIDERS OF THE WORLD.

Programme

OVERTURE, "Star Spangled Banner" - - COWBOY BAND, WM. SWEENY, Leader

1 - **GRAND REVIEW** introducing the Rough Riders of the World and Fully Equipped Regular Soldiers of the Armies of America, England, France, Germany, and Russia.

2 **MISS ANNIE OAKLEY**, Celebrated Shot, who will illustrate her dexterity in the use of Fire-arms.

3 **HORSE RACE** between a Cowboy, a Cossack, a Mexican, an Arab, and an Indian, on Spanish-Mexican, Broncho, Russian, Indian and Arabian Horses.

4 –**PONY EXPRESS.** The Former Pony Post Rider will show how the Letters and Telegrams of the Republic were distributed across the immense Continent previous to the Railways and the Telegraph.

5 –**ILLUSTRATING A PRAIRIE EMIGRANT TRAIN CROSSING THE PLAINS.** Attack by marauding Indians repulsed by "Buffalo Bill," with Scouts and Cowboys.
N. B.—The Wagons are the same as used 35 years ago.

6—**A GROUP OF SYRIAN AND ARABIAN HORSEMEN** will illustrate their style of Horsemanship, with Native Sports and Pastimes.

7—**COSSACKS,** of the Caucasus of Russia, in Feats of Horsemanship, Native Dances, etc.

8—**JOHNNY BAKER,** Celebrated Young American Marksman.

9 – **A GROUP OF MEXICANS** from Old Mexico, will illustrate the use of the Lasso, and perform various Feats of Horsemanship,

10 – **RACING BETWEEN PRAIRIE, SPANISH AND INDIAN GIRLS.**

11—**COWBOY FUN.** Picking Objects from the Ground, Lassoing Wild Horses, Riding the Buckers.

12 –**MILITARY EVOLUTIONS** by a Company of the Sixth Cavalry of the United States Army; a Company of the First Guard Uhlan Regiment of His Majesty King William II, German Emperor, popularly known as the "Potsdamer Reds"; a Company of French Chasseurs (Chasseurs a Cheval de la Garde Republique Francaise); and a Company of the 12th Lancers (Prince of Wales' Regiment) of the British Army.

13 **CAPTURE OF THE DEADWOOD MAIL COACH BY THE INDIANS,** which will be rescued by "Buffalo Bill" and his attendant Cowboys.
N. B.—This is the identical old Deadwood Coach, called the Mail Coach, which is famous on account of having carried the great number of people who lost their lives on the road between Deadwood and Cheyenne 18 years ago. Now the most famed vehicle extant.

14 **RACING BETWEEN INDIAN BOYS ON BAREBACK HORSES.**

15 **LIFE CUSTOMS OF THE INDIANS.** Indian Settlement on the Field and "Path."

16 **COL. W. F. CODY,** ("Buffalo Bill"), in his Unique Feats of Sharpshooting.

17 - **BUFFALO HUNT,** as it is in the Far West of North America—"Buffalo Bill" and Indians. The last of the only known Native Herd.

18 –**THE BATTLE OF THE LITTLE BIG HORN,** Showing with Historical Accuracy the scene of CUSTER'S LAST CHARGE.

19 **SALUTE.**

CONCLUSION.

CAMP AT NOTTINGHAM—AS WILD WEST TRAVELED IN THE PROVINCES OF EUROPE

SALUTATORY.

There is probably no field in modern American history more fascinating in the intensity of its interest than that which is presented in our rapidly-extending frontier. The pressure of the white man, the movement of the emigrant train, and the extension of our railways, together with the military power of the General Government, have, in a measure, broken down the barriers behind which the Indian fought and defied the advance of civilization; but the West, in many places, is still a scene of wildness, where the sternness of law is upheld at the pistol point, and the white savage and outlaw has become scarcely less dangerous than his red-skinned predecessor. (*This last, while perfectly true when written* (1883), *is at present inapplicable, so fast does law and order progress and pervade the Grand West.*

The story of our country, so far as it concerns life in the vast Rocky Mountain region and on the plains, has never been half told; and romance itself falls far short of the reality when it attempts to depict the career of the little vanguard of pioneers, trappers, and scouts, who, moving always in front, have paved the way—frequently with their own bodies—for the safe approach of the masses behind. The names of "OLD JIM BRIDGER," "KIT CARSON," "WHITE BEAVER," "WILD BILL," "CALIFORNIA JOE," "BUFFALO WHITE," "TEXAS JACK," "BUFFALO BILL," MAJOR NORTH, and scores of others, have already become identified with what seem to be strange legends and traditions, and yet the lives and labors of these men form a part of the development of the great West. Most of them have died fighting bravely, and all of them, in their way, have been men around whose exploits contemporaneous writers in and out of the army have thrown the halo of heroism. Our most distinguished officers have repeatedly borne tribute to their usefulness and valor, and to-day the adventures of the Army Scout constitute a theme of never-ending interest. Keen of eye, sturdy in build, inured to hardship, experienced in the knowledge of Indian habits and language, familiar with the hunt, and trustworthy in the hour of extremest danger, they belong to a class that is rapidly disappearing from our country.

In the Eastern States, or even east of the Mississippi, the methods of these people are comparatively unknown, and it is for the purpose of introducing them to the public that this little pamphlet has been prepared. HON. WILLIAM F. CODY ("BUFFALO BILL"), in conjunction with MR. NATE SALSBURY, the eminent American actor (a ranch owner), has organized a large combination that, in its several aspects, will illustrate life as it is witnessed on the plains; the Indian encampment; the cowboys and vaqueros; the herds of buffalo and elk; the lassoing of animals; the manner of robbing mail coaches; feats of agility, horsemanship, marksmanship, archery, and the kindred scenes and events that are characteristic of the border. The most completely appointed delegation of frontiersmen and Indians that ever visited the East will take part in the entertainment, together with a large number of animals; and the performance, while in no wise partaking of the nature of a "circus," will be at once new, startling, and instructive.

JOHN M. BURKE,
General Manager.

NORTH PLATTE, NEB., MAY 1, 1883.

The exhibitions given by "BUFFALO BILL'S" Wild West have nothing in common with the usual professional exhibitions. Their merits are dependent on training of a natural kind.

Our aim is to make the public acquainted with the manners and customs of the daily life of the dwellers in the far West of the United States, through the means of actual and realistic scenes from life. At each performance marked skill and daring are presented. Not only from the standpoint of the spectator, but also from a critical point of view, we assure the auditor that each scene presents a faithful picture of the habits of these folk, down to the smallest detail.

All the horses are descendants of those brought to America by the Spaniards, under Ferdinand Cortez. The whole material of harness, etc., is genuine, and has already been seasoned by many years' experienced use in their original wilds. We congratulate ourselves as being the first to successfully unite in an entertainment all their historic peculiarities.

After having earned the applause of the public and the flattering opinion of the press of the world, New York, London, Paris, Barcelona, Naples, Rome, Milan, Vienna, Munich, Dresden, Leipsic, Berlin, Liverpool, Cardif, Hamburg, Glasgow, Bremen, Brussels, etc., we have the honor to place ourselves once more at the service of the American public, presenting in conjunction with the original Wild West features, a congress of the Rough Riders of the World. This assemblage of primitive horsemen meet for the *first time* in history—from far distant countries—differing in race, language, habits, customs, dress, as well as in skill, style and methods of horsemanship, forming the most unique congregation of equestrians since the creation.

NATE SALSBURY, *Vice-President and Manager.*

HON. W. F. CODY—("BUFFALO BILL"),

Was born in Scott County, Iowa, from whence his father, Isaac Cody, emigrated a few years afterward to the distant frontier territory of Kansas, settling near Fort Leavenworth. While still a boy his father was killed in what is now known as the "Border War," and his youth was passed amid all the excitements and turmoil incident to the strife and discord of that unsettled community, where the embers of political contentions smoldered until they burst into the burning flame of civil war. This state of affairs among the white occupants of the territory, and the ingrained ferocity and hostility to encroachment from the native savage, created an atmosphere of adventure well calculated to educate one of his natural temperament to a familiarity with danger, and self-reliance in the protective means for its avoidance.

From a child used to shooting and riding, he at an early age became a celebrated pony-express rider, then the most dangerous occupation on the plains. He was known as a boy to be most fearless and ready for any mission of danger, and respected by such men then engaged in the express service as Old Jule and the terrible Slade, whose correct finale is truthfully told in Mark Twain's "Roughing It." He accompanied General Albert Sidney Johnston on his Utah expedition, guided trains overland, hunted for a living, and gained his sobriquet by wresting the laurels as a buffalo hunter from all claimants — notably Comstock, in a contest with whom he killed sixty-nine buffalo in one day to Comstock's forty-six —became scout and guide for the now celebrated Fifth Cavalry (of which General E.A. Carr was Major), and is thoroughly identified with that regiment's Western history; was chosen by the Kansas Pacific Railroad to supply meat to the laborers while building the road, in one season killing 4,862 buffaloes, besides deer and antelope; and was chief of scouts in the department that protected the building of the Union Pacific. In these various duties his encounters with the red

men have been innumerable, and are well authenticated by army officers in every section of the country. In fact, wherever you meet an army officer, there you meet an admirer and indorser of Buffalo Bill. He is, in fact, the representative man of the frontiersmen of the past—that is, not the bar-room brawler or bully of the settlements, but a genuine specimen of Western manhood—a child of the plains, who was raised there, and familiar with the country previous to railroads, and when it was known on our maps as the "Great American Desert." By the accident of birth and early association, a man who became sensibly innured to the hardships and dangers of primitive existence, and possessed of those qualities that afterward enabled him to hold positions of trust, and, without his knowing or intending it, made him nationally famous.

Gen. Richard Irving Dodge, Gen. Sherman's chief of staff, correctly states in his "Thirty Years Among Our Wild Indians": "The success of every expedition against Indians depends, to a degree, on the skill, fidelity, and intelligence of the men employed as scouts, for not only is the command habitually dependent on them for good routes and comfortable camps, but the officer in command must rely on them almost entirely for their knowledge of the position and movements of the enemy."

Therefore, besides mere personal bravery, a scout must possess the moral qualities associated with a good captain of a ship—full of self-reliance in his own ability to meet and overcome any unlooked-for difficulties, be a thorough student of nature, a self-taught weather-prophet, a geologist by experience, an astronomer by necessity, a naturalist, and thoroughly educated in the warfare, stratagems, trickery, and skill of his implacable Indian foe. Because, in handling expeditions or leading troops, on him alone depends correctness of destination, avoidance of dangers, protection against sudden storms, the finding of game, grass, wood, and water, the lack of which, of course, is more fatal than the deadly bullet. In fact, more lives have been lost on the plains from incompetent guides than ever the Sioux or Pawnees destroyed.

Our best Indian-fighting officers are quick to recognize these traits in those claiming frontier lore, and to no one in the military history of the West has such deference been shown by them as to W. F. Cody, as is witnessed by the continuous years of service he has passed, the different commands he has served, the expeditions and campaigns he has been identified with, his repeated holding, when he desired, the position of "Chief of Scouts of United States Army," and the intimate associations and contact resulting from it with Gen. W. T. Sherman (with whom he was at the making of the Comanche and Kiowa Treaty), Gen. Phil. Sheridan (who has often given him special recognition and chosen him to organize expeditions, notably that of the Duke Alexis), old Gen. Harney, Gens. W. S. Hancock, Crook, Pope, Miles, Ord, Augur, Terry, McKenzie, Carr, Forsythe, Merritt, Brisbin, Emory, Gibbon, Royal, Hazen, Duncan, Palmer, Pembroke, and the late lamented Gen. Custer. His history, in fact, would be almost a history of the middle West, and, though younger, equaling in term of service and in personal adventure Kit Carson, old Jim Bridger, California Joe, Wild Bill, and the rest of his dead-and-gone associates.

As another evidence of the confidence placed in his frontiersmanship, it may suffice to mention the celebrities whose money and position most naturally sought the best protection the Western market could afford, and who chose to place their lives in his keeping: Sir George Gore, Earl Dunraven, James Gordon Bennett, Duke Alexis, Gen. Custer, Lawrence Jerome, Remington, Professor Ward of Rochester, Professor Marsh of Yale College, Major J. G. Hecksher, Dr. Kingsley (Canon Kingsley's brother), and others of equal rank and distinction. All books of the plains, his exploits with Carr, Miles, and Crook, published in the New York *Herald* and *Times* in the summer of 1876, when he killed Yellow Hand in front of the military command in an open-handed fight, are recorded references.

The following letter of his old commander and celebrated Indian-fighter, Gen. E. A. Carr, written years ago relative to him, is a tribute as generous as any brave man has ever made to one of his position:

"From his services with my command, steadily in the field, I am qualified to bear testimony as to his qualities and character.

"He was very modest and unassuming. He is a natural gentleman in his manners as well as in character, and has none of the roughness of the typical frontiersman. He can take his own part when required, but I have never heard of his using a knife or a pistol, or engaging in a quarrel where it could be avoided. His personal strength and activity are very great, and his temper and disposition are so good that no one has reason to quarrel with him.

"His eyesight is better than a good field-glass; he is the best trailer I ever heard of, and also the best judge of the 'lay of country'—that is, he is able to tell what kind of country is ahead, so as to know how to act. He is a perfect judge of distance, and always ready to tell correctly how many miles it is to water, or to any place, or how many miles have been marched.

"Mr. Cody seemed never to tire and was always ready to go, in the darkest night, or the worst weather, and usually volunteered, knowing what the emergency required. His trailing, when following Indians, or looking for stray animals or for game, is simply wonderful. He is a most extraordinary hunter.

"In a fight Mr. Cody is never noisy, obstreperous or excited. In fact, I never hardly noticed him in a fight, unless I happened to want him, or he had something to report, when he was always in the right place, and his information was always valuable and reliable.

"During the winter of 1866 we encountered hardships and exposure in terrific snowstorms, sleet, etc., etc. On one occasion that winter Mr. Cody showed his quality by quietly offering to go with some dispatches to Gen. Sheridan, across a dangerous region, where another principal scout was reluctant to risk himself.

"Mr. Cody has since served with me as post guide and scout at Fort McPherson, where he frequently distinguished himself. * * *

"In the summer of 1876 Cody went with me to the Black Hills region, where he killed Yellow Hand. Afterward he was with the Big Horn and Yellowstone expedition. I consider that his services to the country and the army by trailing, finding and fighting Indians, and thus protecting the frontier settlers, and by guiding commands over the best and most practicable routes, have been invaluable."

Thus it will be seen that, notwithstanding it may sometimes be thought his fame rests upon

7

the pen of the romancer and novelist, had they never been attracted to him (and they were solely by his sterling worth), W. F. CODY would none the less have been a character in American history. Having assisted in founding substantial peace in Nebraska, where he was honored by being elected to the legislature (while away on a hunt), he has settled at North Platte, to enjoy the fruits and minister to the wants and advancements of the domestic circle with which he is blessed. On the return to civil life of his old prairie friend, Major North, in rehearsing the old time years agone on the Platte, the Republican, and the Medicine, they concluded to reproduce some of the interesting scenes on the plains and in the Wild West.

The history of such a man, attractive as it already has been to the most distinguished officers and fighters in the United States Army, must prove doubly so to the men, women, and children who have heretofore found only in the novel the hero of rare exploits, on which imagination so loves to dwell. Young, sturdy, a remarkable specimen of manly beauty, with the brain to conceive and the nerve to execute, Buffalo Bill *par excellence* is the exemplar of the strong and unique traits that characterize *a true American frontiersman.*

ACROSS THE CONTINENT WITH THE FIFTH CAVALRY.

Captain George F. Price's history of this famous regiment recounts its experience from the time it was known as the Second Dragoons to the present, giving the historical record of its officers, among whom are numbered many of the most distinguished military leaders known in our national annals, such as Gen. Albert Sydney Johnston, Gen. George H. Thomas, Gen. Robert E. Lee, Gen. John Sedgwick, Gens. Hardee, Emory, Van Dorn, Merritt, Carr, Royall, Custer, and others of equal note. Besides alluding in many of its pages to incidents, adventures, and conduct of the favorite guide and scout of the regiment, W. F. CODY ("BUFFALO BILL"), Captain Price completes a narrative of brave men and daring deeds by "flood and field" with the following biographical sketch (page 583) of W. F. CODY, "BUFFALO BILL."

W. F. CODY—("BUFFALO BILL").

"WILLIAM F. CODY was born in Scott County, Iowa. He removed at an early age to Kansas, and was employed as a herder, wagonmaster, and pony express rider. He went to Pike's Peak during the excitement which followed the discovery of gold in Colorado, but failing of success, returned to Kansas and became a trapper on the Republican River. In the fall of 1861 he was a Government scout and guide at Fort Larned, Kan., and in 1862 served as a scout and guide for the Ninth Kansas Cavalry, being chiefly employed in Arkansas and Southwestern Missouri. In 1863 he enlisted in the Seventh Kansas Cavalry, and served in Tennessee, Mississippi, Missouri, and Kansas, and participated in several battles. He was made a non-commissioned officer, and served as a scout for his regiment after the battle of Tupelo. He was honorably discharged at the end of the war, and engaged in various business pursuits until the spring of 1867, when he made a contract, for a monthly compensation of five hundred dollars, to deliver all the buffalo meat that would be needed for food purposes for a number of laborers on the Kansas Pacific Railway in Western Kansas, and during this engagement—a period of less than eighteen months—he killed four thousand two hundred and eighty buffaloes. This remarkable success gained for him the name of 'Buffalo Bill.' When hunting buffalo, Cody would ride his horse, whenever possible, to the right front of a herd, shoot down the leaders, and crowd their followers to the left until they began to run in a circle, when he would soon kill all that he required. Cody again entered the Government service in 1868 as a scout and guide, and, after a series of dangerous rides as bearer of important dispatches through a country which was infested with hostile Indians, was appointed by General Sheridan chief scout and guide for the Fifth Cavalry, which had been recently ordered from reconstruction duty in the Southern States for a campaign against the hostile Sioux and Cheyennes. He joined a detachment of the regiment at Fort Hays, Kansas, and was engaged, during the fall of 1868, in the combats on Beaver and Shuter Creeks and north branch of Solomon River. He then served with the Canadian River expedition during the winter of 1868-69, and became deservedly conspicuous for cheerful service under dispiriting circumstances, and the successful discharge of important duties. He marched with a battalion of the regiment across the country from Fort Lyon, Colo., to Fort McPherson, Neb., during May, 1869, and was engaged *en route* in the combat at Beaver Creek, Kan., where he rendered an important and brilliant service by carrying dispatches from a detached party to the cavalry camp after a soldier courier had been driven back by the Indians; and again at Spring Creek, Neb., three days latter, where, when the advance guard under Lieutenant Babcock was surrounded by a large force of the enemy, he was distinguished for coolness and bravery.

BILL CODY—"BUFFALO BILL," THE SCOUT.

"Cody was appointed chief scout and guide for the Republican River expedition of 1869, and was conspicuous during the pursuit of the Dog Soldiers, under the celebrated Cheyenne chief, Tall Bull, to Summit Springs, Colo. He also guided the Fifth Cavalry to a position whence the Regiment was enabled to charge upon the enemy, and win a brilliant victory. He afterward participated in the Niobrara pursuit, and later narrowly escaped death at the hands of hostile Sioux on Prairie Dog Creek, Kan., September 26, 1869. He was assigned to Fort McPherson when the expedition was disbanded, and served at that station (was a Justice of the Peace in 1871) until the Fifth Cavalry was transferred to Arizona. He served during this period with several expeditions, and was conspicuous for gallant conduct in the Indian combat at Red Willow and Birdwood Creeks, and also for successful services as chief scout and guide of the buffalo hunt which was arranged by General Sheridan for the Grand Duke Alexis of Russia.

Cody was then assigned to duty with the Third Cavalry, and served with that regiment until the fall of 1872, when he was elected a member of the Nebraska Legislature, and thus acquired the title of 'Honorable. But, accepting the advice of Eastern friends, he resigned his seat in the Legislature and also his position of scout and guide at Fort McPherson, and proceeded to Chicago, where he made his first appearance as an actor in a drama entitled 'The Scouts of the Plains,' winning an instant success . . . . .

"At the beginning of the Sioux War in 1876, he hastened to Cheyenne, Wyo., joined the Fifth Cavalry, which has recently returned from Arizona, and was engaged in the affair at War Bonnet (Indian Creek), Wyo., where he killed in a hand-to-hand combat the Cheyenne Chief, Yellow Hand. He then accompanied the Fifth Cavalry to Goose Creek, Mont., and served with the Big Horn and Yellowstone expedition until September, when business engagements compelled him to return to the Eastern States. Cody abundantly proved during this campaign that he had lost none of his old-time skill and daring in Indian warfare. He enjoys a brilliant reputation as a scout and guide, which has been fairly earned by faithful and conspicuous service.

"He is modest and unassuming, and free from the common faults of the typical frontiersman. His present lucrative business has made him widely known throughout the country. He has valuable property interests at North Platte, Neb., and is owner of an extensive cattle ranch on Dismal River, 65 miles north of North Platte, having for a partner in the business Major Frank North, who is well-known as the whilom commander of the celebrated Pawnee scouts.

"William F. Cody is one of the best scouts and guides that ever rode at the head of a column of cavalry on the prairies of the Far West. His army friends, from general to private, hope that he may live long and prosper abundantly.

"Should the wild Sioux again go on the war-path, Cody, if living, will be found with the cavalry advance, riding another 'Buckskin Joe,' and carrying his Springfield rifle, 'Lucretia,' across the pommel of his saddle."

FROM COL. DODGE'S "THIRTY YEARS AMONG THE INDIANS."—*Page* 628.

"Of ten men employed as scouts nine will prove to be worthless; of fifty so employed one may prove to be really valuable, but, though hundreds, even thousands of men have been so employed by the Government since the war, the number of really remarkable men among them can be counted on the fingers. The services which these men are called on to perform are so important and valuable that the officer who benefits by them is sure to give the fullest credit, and men honored in official reports come to be great men on the frontier. Fremont's reports made Kit Carson a renowned man. Custer immortalized California Joe. Custer, Merritt, and Carr made William F. Cody (Buffalo Bill) a plains celebrity 'UNTIL TIME SHALL BE NO MORE.'"

A Legislator.—The late Phocian Howard journalistically records the fact:—"We were present in the Nebraska Legislature when Mr. Cody's resignation was read, and knowing his practical qualities, his thorough knowledge of important questions then demanding attention in border legislation, his acquaintance with the Indian problem—the savage's deadly foe in battle, their generous friend in peace—great was our disappointment in his refusing to continue in political life, choosing to be, what he really is, a true 'Knight of the Plains.' On the frontier, even there his name a household word, deservedly is the famous scout popular throughout the land, standing, as he has, a leader among the manly pioneer barriers between civilization and savagery, risking all, that the 'Star of Empire might force its westward way.' We know Bill Cody well, having been with him in three campaigns among the Indians, the last being the memorable Custer campaign under Crook, on the Big Horn, against the Sitting Bull Sioux, and we bear kind witness that Buffalo Bill is the idol of the army and frontiersmen, and the dread and terror of the war-bonneted Indian. At the last session of the Nebraska Legislature he received a large complimentary vote for United States Senator."

A Pen Picture.—Curtis Guild proprietor and editor of the Conservative *Commercial Bulletin*, Boston, writes—"Raised on the frontier, he has passed through every grade, and won fame in each line, while to be proficient in one brings celebrity sufficient to gratify most ambitions. Thus it is he holds supremacy in fact, and receives from his associates an adoration surpassing even his public popularity. Visitors to the camp, early the other morning, found him joining in every frolic, game, and contest, with each and all, and generally excelling; in shooting, in running, in jumping, in trials of strength, feats of agility, horsemanship, handling the ribbons behind four or six, riding the vicious mustang, manipulating the revolver, etc., tackling each specialist, and coming to the front with a generous modesty admired by the defeated.

"No lover of the human race, no man with an eye for the picturesque, but must have enjoyed the very sight of these pioneers of civilization. Never was a finer picture of American manhood presented than when Buffalo Bill stepped out to show the capabilities of the Western teamster's whip. Tall beyond the lot of ordinary mortals, straight as an arrow, not an ounce of useless flesh upon his limbs, but every muscle firm and hard as the sinews of a stag, with the frank, kindly eye of a devoted friend, and a natural courtly grace of manner which would become a marshal of France, Buffalo Bill is from spur to sombrero one of the finest types of manhood this continent has ever produced. Those who had expected to meet a different class of men must have been pleasantly surprised in these genuine sons of the plains every one of whom was stamped with the natural easy grace and courtesy of manner which marks the man who is born a gentleman."

As an Educator.—The nationally known Brick Pomeroy thus writes:—"One of the pronounced, positive, strong men of the West is Hon. Wm. F. Cody, of Nebraska, known quite generally the world over as 'Buffalo Bill.' A sturdy, generous, positive character, who, as hunter, guide, scout, Government officer, member of the Legislature, and gentleman, rises to the equal of every emergency into which his way is opened or directed. Quick to think and to act, cool in all cases of pleasure or extreme danger; versatile in his genius; broad and liberal in his ideas; progressive in his mentality, he can no more keep still or settle down into a routine work incidental to office or farm life, than an eagle can thrive in a cage.

"The true Western man is free, fearless, generous and chivalrous. Of this class, Hon. Wm. F. Cody, 'Buffalo Bill,' is a bright representative. As a part of his rushing career he has brought together material for what he correctly terms a Wild West Exhibition. I should call it a Wild West Reality. The idea is not merely to take in money from those who witness a very lively exhibition, but to give people in the East a correct representation of life on the plains, and the incidental life of the hardy, brave, intelligent pioneers, who are the first to blaze the way to the future homes and greatness of America. He knows the worth and sturdiness of true Western character, and as a lover of his country, wishes to present as many facts as possible to the public, so that those who will, can see actual pictures of life in the West, brought to the East for the inspection and education of the public.

"'Buffalo Bill' has brought the Wild West to the doors of the East. There is more of real life, of genuine interest, of positive education in this startling exhibition, than I have ever before seen, and it is as true to nature and life as it really is with those who are smoothing the way for millions to follow. All of this imaginary Romeo and Juliet business sinks to utter insignificance in comparison to the drama of existence as is here so well enacted, and all the operas in the world appear like pretty playthings for emasculated children by the side of the setting of reality, and the music of the frontier as so faithfully and extensively presented, and so cleverly managed by this incomparable representative of Western pluck, coolness, bravery, independence, and generosity. I wish every person east of the Missouri River could only see this true, graphic picture of wild Western life, they would know more and think better of the genuine men of the West.

"I wish there were more progresssive educators like Wm. F. Cody in this world.

"He deserves well for his efforts to please and to instruct in matters important to America, and incidents that are passing away *never more to return.*"

Could a man now living have stood on the shore of the Red Sea, and witnessed the passage of the children of Israel and the struggle of Pharaoh and his hosts, what a sight he would have seen, and how interested would be those to whom he related the story. Could the man who stood on the shore to see Washington and his soldiers cross the Delaware have lived till now to tell the story, what crowds he would have to listen. How interesting would be the story of a man, if he were now living, that had witnessed the landing of Columbus on the shores of the New World; or the story of one of the hardy English Puritans who took passage on the "Mayflower," and landed on the rock-bound coast of New England.

THE FORMER FOE—PRESENT FRIEND, THE AMERICAN.

So, too, of the angel who has seen the far West become tame and dotted under advancing civilization, as the pioneers fought their way westward into desert and jungle. What a story he can relate as to the making of that history. And what a history America has, to be sure! From the mouth of the Hudson River to the shores of the Pacific, men, women and children have conquered the wilderness by going to the front and staying there. Not by crowding into cities and living as do worms, by crawling through each other and devouring the leavings.

Since the railroad gave its aid to pioneering, America is making history faster than any other country in the world. *Her pioneers are fast passing away.* A few years more and the great struggle for possession will be ended, and generations will settle down to enjoy the homes their fathers located and fenced in for them. Then will come the picture maker. He who, with pen, pencil, and panel, can tell the story as he understands it. Then millions will read and look at what the pioneer did and what the historian related, wishing the while that they could have been there to have seen the original. These are of the thoughts to crowd in upon us as we view the great living picture that the Hon. Wm. F. Cody ("Buffalo Bill") gives at the Wild West Exhibition, which every man, woman and child the world over should see and study as a realistic fact.

We see audiences of thousands each night—statesmen, artists, military men, teachers, workers, musicians, business men, politicians, artisans, mechanics, and others who desire to know as much as possible of the history of America.

We see "Buffalo Bill," the last of the six greatest scouts this country has ever known, viz., Boone, Crockett, Carson, Bridger, "Wild Bill," and "Buffalo Bill," and to our mind the greatest and most remarkable of all—a man whom this country will never duplicate. A nonesuch to the credit of Nature, the world, and the mental and physical material of which he was formed, as one made to do a certain great work. A man in the prime of life, who, from the age of ten years, has fought fate and all adverse circumstances, and never to a loss. A man who is a man; as a scout; as a pioneer; as a Government officer; as an Indian fighter; as a mighty hunter; as a man of honor, and of more than ordinary skill and courage, commanding admiration—deserving of recognition as a great character in American history. A natural man of the highest order.—*Editorial, New York Democrat, June 5, 1886.*

OLD TIME CAMP IN THE WILD WEST; OR, ON THE PLATTE IN 1857.

BUFFALO BILL AT HOME.—His Great Success Abroad.

"North Platte should be congratulated on the possession of a citizen whose prominence or position is not bounded by his township, his country, or his State, but whose name is a household word, whose pictures are familiar, and whose character is known, not only throughout the nation, but has adorned pages, and interested the readers of foreign works and publications. We allude to our fellow citizen, Hon. W. F. Cody, whose sobriquet of 'Buffalo Bill' represents a popularity only bounded by the area of American territory, and to which we, who live by his own fireside, may testify his worthy possession and to the modesty of its wearing. His late return from a successful presentation to the East of some of the animated daily scenes and incidents that go to form the passing history of 'The Wild West' should be noted, as are events of importance, as it marks a new era in the history of amusements: that for originality, adherence to truth in 'holding the mirror up to Nature,' and a fidelity to fact that is the 'true aim of art.' The reception accorded to his 'show that is not a show, but an illustration,' in the cultured cities of the East, notably Boston, Chicago, Newport, New York, Philadelphia, Cincinnati and Cleveland, must be gratifying to all in North Platte, in fact in Nebraska, where, in the incipiency of the scheme, over a year ago, he demonstrated by courage, pluck and perseverance, its feasibility by its introduction in the festivities of our national birthday celebration, and on the following natal day presented it on the shores of the Atlantic, to the plaudits of over 25,000 delighted Bostonians. The magnitude of the undertaking, the minutiæ necessary to organizing, the bringing together from all points the best marksmen in the world, securing admirable and fitting representatives of the cattle trade, getting wild buffalo, elk, steers, mules, ponies, specimens of the red terrors of the prairie, and other features of interest known only to the pampas of the West, necessitating special trains of cars for transportation, and driving the strange cavalcade through confined Washington Street, Boston, in six weeks after leaving the Platte, was an accomplishment that stamps Cody as a wonder in energy, and gained for him the admiration and encomiums from the entire press of the East, recognition from the *elite* of American society, encouragement from representatives of education, and the indorsement of his methods by the S. P. C. A. and its noted president, Professor Henry Berg."—*North Platte Telegraph*, 1884.

CODY'S CORRAL; OR, THE SCOUTS AND THE SIOUX.

By "Buckskin Sam."

A mount-inclosed valley, close sprinkled with fair flowers,
As if a shattered rainbow had fallen there in showers;
Bright-plumaged birds were warbling their songs among the trees,
Or fluttering their tiny wings in the cooling western breeze.
The cottonwoods, by mountain's base, on every side high tower,
And the dreamy haze in silence marks the sleepy noontide hour.
East, south and north, to meet the clouds the lofty mounts arise,
Guarding this little valley—a wild Western Paradise.
Pure and untrampled as it looks, this lovely flower-strewn sod—
One scarce would think that e'er, by man, had such a sward been trod;
But yonder, see those wild mustangs by lariat held in check,
Tearing up the fairest flora, which fairies might bedeck;
And, near a camp-fire's smoke, we see men standing all around—
'Tis strange, for from them has not come a single word or sound.
Standing by cottonwood, with arms close-folded on his breast,
Gazing with his eagle eyes up to the mountain's crest,
Tall and commanding is his form, and graceful is his mien;
As fair in face, as noble, has seldom here been seen.
A score or more of frontiersmen recline upon the ground,
But starting soon upon their feet, by sudden snort and bound!
A horse has sure been frightened by strange scent on the breeze,
And glances now by all are cast beneath the towering trees.
A quiet sign their leader gives, and mustangs now are brought;
And, by swift-circling lasso, a loose one fast is caught.
Then thundering round the mountain's dark adamantine side,
A hundred hideous, painted, and fierce Sioux warriors ride;
While, from their throats, the well-known and horrible death-knell
The wild blood-curdling war-whoop, and the fierce and fiendish yell,
Strikes the ears of all, now ready to fight, and e'en to die,
In that mount-inclosed valley, beneath that blood-red sky!
Now rings throughout the open, on all sides clear and shrill,
The dreaded battle-cry of him whom men call Buffalo Bill!
On, like a whirlwind, then they dash—the brave scouts of the plains,
Their rifle-barrels soft-carest by mustang's flying manes!
On, like an avalanche, they sweep through the tall prairie grass;
Down, fast upon them, swooping, the dread and savage mass!
Wild yells of fierce bravado come, and taunts of deep despair;
While, through the battle-smoke there flaunts each feathered tuft of hair.
And loudly rings the war-cry of fearless Buffalo Bill;
And loudly rings the savage yells, which make the blood run chill!
The gurgling death cry mingles with the mustang's shrillest scream.
And sound of dull and sodden falls and bowie's brightest gleam.
At length there slowly rises the smoke from heaps of slain,
Whose wild war-cries will never more ring on the air again.
Then, panting and bespattered from the showers of foam and blood,
The scouts have once more halted 'neath the shady cottonwood.
In haste they are re-loading, and preparing for a sally,
While the scattered foe, now desperate, are yelling in the valley.
Again are heard revolvers, with their rattling, sharp report;
Again the scouts are seen to charge down on that wild cohort
Sioux fall around, like dead reeds, when fiercest northers blow,
And rapid sink in death before their hated pale-face foe!
Sad, smothered now is music from the mountain's rippling rill,
But wild hurrahs instead are heard from our brave Buffalo Bill,
Who, through the thickest carnage charged ever in the van,
And cheered faint hearts around him, since first the fight began
Deeply demoralized, the Sioux fly fast with bated breath,
And glances cast of terror along that vale of death;
While the victors quick dismounted, and looking all around,
On their dead and mangled enemies, whose corses strewed the ground,
"I had sworn I would avenge them"--were the words of Buffalo Bill-
"The mothers and their infants they slew at Medicine Hill.
Our work is done--done nobly--I looked for that from you;
Boys, when a cause is just, you need but stand firm and true!"

—*Beadle's Weekly.*

A stirring life picture of a battle between the whites and Indians, showing the tactics and mode of warfare of each, will be given by the skilled members of both races in "Buffalo Bill's" representation of scenes in the Wild West.

THE PAWNEES ASTONISHED.

W. F. Cody, although having established his right to the title of "Buffalo Bill" for years before, had not had opportunity to convince the Pawnees of the justice of the claim previous to the time of the following incident. A short while previously a band of marauding red-skin renegades from that nation, while on a stealing excursion near Ellsworth, had occasion to regret their temerity, and cause to remember him to the extent of three killed, which fact for a time resulted in an enmity that needed something out of the usual run to establish him in their favor. While on a military expedition, under Gen. E. A. Carr, upon the Republican, he met Major North and the Pawnee scouts. One day a herd of buffalo were descried, and CODY desired to join in the hunt. The Indians objected, telling the Major, "The white talker would only scare them away." Seventy-three Indians attacked the herd and killed twenty-three. Later in the day another herd was discovered, and Major North insisted that the white chief have a chance to prove his skill. After much grumbling, they acquiesced grudgingly, and with ill-concealed smiles of derision consented to be spectators. Judge of their surprise when CODY charged the herd, and single-handed and alone fairly amazed them by killing forty-eight buffalo in fifty minutes, thus forever gaining their admiration and a firm friendship that has since often accrued to his benefit.

COLONEL ROYALL'S WAGONS.

Once upon the South Fork of the Solomon, Col. Royall ordered CODY to kill some buffalo that were in sight to feed his men, but declined to send his wagons until assured of the game. Bill rounded the herd, and, getting them in a line for camp, drove them in and killed seven near headquarters; or, as the Colonel afterward laughingly remarked, "furnishing grub and his own transportation."

THE BOW AND ARROW.

The bow is the natural weapon of the wild tribes of the West. Previous to the introduction of fire-arms, it was the weapon supreme of every savage's outfit—in fact, his principal dependence, backed by personal skill in its use, for sustenance for himself and his pappooses. It still retains its favor, as it is not always safe to rely on the white man's mechanism, as in case of lack of ammunition or deranged lock or trigger, time and location prevent its being "mended." As a weapon of economy, it is also to be commended, as the hunting arrow is made so that the rear shoulders of the long, tapering blade slope backward, thus facilitating its withdrawal from the wounded game. On the other hand, in the war arrow, the rear shoulders slope forward, forming barbs, as it is intended to remain and eventually kill. The possession, therefore, of firearms has not affected the Indian's love of this reliable weapon of the chase, which, being his first childish plaything, is still, no matter how well armed or how rich he may be, an indispensable possession. At short distances it is a terribly effective arm, and the Indian expert can seize five to ten arrows in his left hand, and dispatch them with such rapidity that the last one will be on its flight before the first one touches the ground. In close quarters they prefer to rely on it to depending on the rifle, as it can be of deadly force at from thirty to forty yards, and creating a bad wound at much greater distance. In buffalo hunting, where the horseman can approach near, it is invaluable and economic, and is often buried to the feathers. "Two Lance," an Indian chief, during the Grand Duke's hunt, sent an arrow clear through a bison, Alexis retaining the light-winged messenger of death as a souvenir of his hunt on the American Plains.

THE BUFFALO.

The buffalo is the true bison of the ancients. It is distinguished by an elevated stature, measuring six to seven feet at the shoulders, and ten to twelve feet from nose to tail. Many are under the impression that the buffalo was never an inhabitant of any country save ours. Their bones have been discovered in the superficial strata of temperate Europe; they were common in Germany in the eighth century. Primitive man in America found this animal his principal means of subsistence, while to pioneers, hunters, emigrants, settlers, and railroad builders this fast disappearing monarch of the plains was invaluable. MESSRS. CODY & Co. have a herd of healthy specimens of this hardy bovine in connection with their instructive exhibition, "The Wild West," rendered interesting as the last of their kind.

A PRACTICAL "ALL-ROUND SHOT."

In contradistinction to the many so-called "fancy shots" that have for years been before the public, "BUFFALO BILL" is what may be termed a "practical marksman," and where that expression's full meaning is understood, he is looked on as a marvelous "all-round shot." That is, a man of deadly aim in any emergency, with any weapon—a small Derringer, a Colt's, a shot-gun, a carbine, a blunderbus, or a rifle—at any foe, red or white; at any game—chicken, jack-rabbit, antelope, deer, buffalo, bear, or elk; at the swiftest bird or soaring eagle; on foot, in any position; on horseback, at any speed. To be such a marksman is only the result of years of necessity for exercising the faculties of instantaneous measurement of distance, acuteness of vision—in fact, an eagle eye and iron nerves—to think quick, to resolve, to fire, to kill. As a hunter these gifts have rendered him famous and gained him plaudits from admiring officers, noblemen, sportsmen, and competitors in the chase, and compelled the respect and fear of his implacable Indian foes. That he exists to-day is the result of the training that enables a man in the most startling exigency to command himself, and to meet the circumstances face to face, whatever they may be, and achieve, by cool precision, deserved victory in the field, and embellish history with deeds of heroism. MR. CODY will give an exhibition of his ability by shooting objects thrown in the air while galloping at full speed, executing difficulties that would receive commendation if accomplished on foot, and which can only be fully appreciated by those who have attempted the feat while experiencing a rapid pace when occupying "a seat in the saddle."

CODY SAVES "WILD BILL."

After a very long march, full of hardships and suffering, Gen. Penrose's camp was found on the Palodora in a most distracted condition. Gen. Carr's arrival was none too soon, as the famished men were sustaining life on the last carcasses of their draught animals. In a few weeks Black Kettle's depredations necessitated a pursuit. . . . The consolidated command discovered the Indians on the Cimarron, and a terrific battle ensued. . . . In this fight "Buffalo Bill" and "Wild Bill" did almost the work of a regiment; braver men never went into an action, both fighting as though they were invulnerable. In the fury and rout which followed the first charge, "WILD BILL" gave chase to Black Kettle, head chief of the Cheyennes, overtook and engaged the fleeing red warrior, stabbing him to death. But the accomplishment of this heroic action would have cost him his own life, had not "BUFFALO BILL" ridden with impetuous daring into the very midst of fully fifty Indians, who had surrounded "WILD BILL," intent on either his capture or death. The two daring and intrepid scouts plunged furiously into the midst of the Indians, each with a revolver in either hand, and literally carved their way through the surging mass of redskins, leaving a furrow of dead Indians in their wake. Such fighting, such riding, and such marvelous intrepidity combined, were doubtless never equaled, and if but this act alone were credited to the valor of "WILD BILL" and "BUFFALO BILL," their names would deserve inscription on Fame's enduring monument.—*Buell's History.*

LETTERS OF COMMENDATION FROM PROMINENT MILITARY MEN.

FROM AN OLD COMMANDER.

[COPY]

5th Avenue Hotel, New York,
June 29th, 1887.

HON. WM. F. CODY,
London, England.

DEAR CODY:—In common with all your countrymen, I want to let you know that I am not only gratified, but proud of your management and general behavior; so far as I can make out you have been modest, graceful, and dignified in all you have done to illustrate the history of civilization on this Continent during the past century.

I am especially pleased with the graceful and pretty compliment paid you by the Princess of Wales, who rode in the Deadwood Coach while it was attacked by the Indians and rescued by the Cowboys. Such things did occur in our days, and may never again.

As near as I can estimate there were *in 1865 about nine and a half of millions of buffaloes* on the plains between the Missouri River and the Rocky Mountains; all are now gone—killed for their meat, their skins and bones.

This seems like desecration, cruelty, and murder, yet they have been replaced by twice as many *neat* cattle. At that date there were about 165,000 *Pawnees, Sioux, Cheyennes, Kiowas, and Arapahoes,* who depended on these buffaloes for their yearly food. They, too, are gone, and have been replaced by twice or thrice as many white men and women, who have made the earth to blossom as the rose, and who can be counted, taxed, and governed by the laws of nature and civilization. This change has been salutary, and will go on to the end. You have caught one epoch of the world's history; have illustrated it in the very heart of the modern world—London, and I want you to feel that on this side the water we appreciate it. This drama must end; days, years, and centuries follow fast, even the drama of civilization must have an end.

All I aim to accomplish on this sheet of paper is to assure you that I fully recognize your work and that the presence of the Queen, the beautiful Princess of Wales, the Prince, and British public, are marks of favor which reflect back on America sparks of light which illuminate many a house and cabin in the land where once *you guided me honestly and faithfully in 1865-'6 from Fort Riley to Kearney in Kansas and Nebraska.* Sincerely your friend, W. T. SHERMAN.

WAR DEPARTMENT, ADJUTANT-GENERAL'S OFFICE,
WASHINGTON, August 10, 1886.

To whom it may concern:

MR. WILLIAM F. CODY was employed as Chief of Scouts under Generals SHERIDAN, CUSTER, CROOK, MILES, CARR, and others, in their campaigns against hostile Indians on our frontier, and as such rendered very valuable and distinguished service. S. W. DRUM, Adjutant-General.

STATE OF NEBRASKA.

To all whom these presents shall come, GREETING:

Know Ye, that, I, JOHN M. THAYER, Governor of the State of Nebraska, reposing special trust and confidence in the integrity, patriotism and ability of the HON. WILLIAM F. CODY, on behalf and in the name of the State, do hereby appoint and commission him as Aide-de-Camp of my Staff, with the rank of Colonel, and do authorize and empower him to discharge the duties of said office according to law.

In testimony whereof I have hereunto subscribed my name and caused to be affixed the Great Seal of the State.

GRAND SEAL OF THE STATE OF NEBRASKA March 1st, 1867.

Done at Lincoln this 8th day of March, A. D., 1867.
JOHN M. THAYER.
By the Governor,
G. L. LAUR, Secretary ot State.

The following letter received with a photograph of the hero of the "March to the Sea," Gen. W. T Sherman:

NEW YORK, December 25, 1886.

To COL. WM. F. CODY:—With the best compliments of one who, in 1866, was guided by him up the Republican, then occupied by the Cheyennes and Arapahoes as their ancestral hunting-grounds, now transformed into farms and cattle-ranches, in better harmony with modern civilization, and with his best wishes that he succeed in his honorable efforts to represent the scenes of that day to a generation then unborn. W. T. SHERMAN, General.

NEW YORK, December 28, 1886.

COL. WM. F. CODY: DEAR SIR,—Recalling the many facts that came to me while I was Adjutant-General of the Division of the Missouri, under General Sheridan, bearing upon your efficiency, fidelity, and daring as a guide and scout over the country west of the Missouri River and east of the Rocky Mountains, I take pleasure in observing your success in depicting in the East the early life of the West. Very truly yours, JAMES B. FRY,
Assistant Adjutant-General, Brevet Major-General, U. S. A

HEADQUARTERS ARMY OF THE UNITED STATES,
WASHINGTON, D. C., January 7, 1887.

COL. WM. F. CODY was a scout, and served in my command on the Western frontier for many years. He was always ready for duty, and was a cool, brave man, with unimpeachable character. I take pleasure in commending him for the many services he has rendered to the Army, whose respect he enjoys for his manly qualities. P. H. SHERIDAN,
Lieutenant-General.

LOS ANGELES, CAL., January 7, 1878.

COL. WM. F. CODY: DEAR SIR,—Having visited your great exhibition in St. Louis and New York City, I desire to congratulate you on the success of your enterprise. I was much interested in the various life-like representations of Western scenery, as well as the fine exhibition of skilled markmanship and magnificent horsemanship. You not only represent the many interesting features of frontier life, but also the difficulties and dangers that have been encountered by the adventurous and fearless pioneers of civilization. The wild Indian life as it was a few years ago will soon be a thing of the past, but you appear to have selected a good class of Indians to represent that race of people, and I regard your Exhibition as not only very interesting but practically instructive. Your services on the frontier were exceedingly valuable. With best wishes for your success, believe me very truly yours,
NELSON A. MILES, Brigadier-General, U. S. A.

"HE IS KING OF THEM ALL."

HEADQUARTERS MOUNTED RECRUITING SERVICE,
ST. LOUIS, MO., May 7, 1885.

MAJOR JOHN M. BURKE: DEAR SIR,—I take pleasure in saying that in an experience of about thirty years on the plains and in the mountains, I have seen a great many guides, scouts, trailers, and hunters, and Buffalo Bill (W. F. Cody) is King of them all. He has been with me in seven Indian fights, and his services have been invaluable. Very respectfully yours,
EUGENE A. CARR, Brevet Major-General, U. S. A.

UNITED STATES MILITARY ACADEMY,
WEST POINT, N. Y., January 11, 1887.

* * * I have known W. F. CODY (Buffalo Bill) for many years. He is a Western man of the best type, combining those qualities of enterprise, daring, good sense, and physical endurance which made him the superior of any scout I ever knew. He was cool and capable when surrounded by dangers, and his reports were always free from exaggeration. He is a gentleman in that better sense of the word which implies character, and he may be depended on under all circumstances. I wish him success.

W. MERRITT, Brevet Major-General, U. S. A.,
Late Major-General Volunteers.

BUFFALO BILL GUIDING GENERAL SHERIDAN'S RELIEF TRAIN IN WINTER, 1868.

OMAHA, NEB., January 7, 1887.

HON. WM. F. CODY: DEAR SIR,—I take great pleasure in testifying to the very efficient service rendered by you "as a scout," in the campaign against the Sioux Indians, during the year 1876. Also, that I have witnessed your Wild West Exhibition. I consider it the most realistic performance of the kind I have ever seen.

Very sincerely, your obedient servant,
GEORGE CROOK, Brigadier-General U. S. A.

WASHINGTON, D. C., February 8, 1887.

MR. CODY was chief guide and hunter to my command, when I commanded the District of North Platte, and he performed all his duties with marked excellence.

W. H. EMORY, Major-General U. S. A.

HEADQUARTERS 7TH CAVALRY, FORT MEAD, DAKOTA TERRITORY,
February 14, 1887.

MY DEAR SIR,—Your army career on the frontier, and your present enterprise of depicting scenes in the Far West, are so enthusiastically approved and commended by the American people and the most prominent men of the U. S. Army, that there is nothing left for me to say. I feel sure your new departure will be a success.

With best wishes, I remain, yours truly,
JAMES W. FORSYTH, Colonel 7th Cavalry.

JERSEY CITY, 405 BERGEN AVE., February 7, 1887.

HON. WM. F. CODY: MY DEAR SIR,—I fully and with pleasure indorse you as th eritable "Buffalo Bill," U. S. Scout, serving with the troops operating against hostile Indians in 1868, on the plains. I speak from personal knowledge, and from reports of officers and others, with whom you secured renown by your services as a scout and successful hunter. Your sojourn on the frontier at a time when it was a wild and sparsely settled section of the Continent, fully enables you to portray that in which I have personally participated—the Pioneer, Indian Fighter, and Frontiersman. Wishing you every success, I remain, very respectfully yours,

H. C. BANKHEAD, Brigadier-General, U. S. A.

HOTEL RICHMOND, WASHINGTON, D. C., January 9, 1887.

W. F. CODY (Buffalo Bill) was with me in the early days, when I commanded a Battalion of the 5th Cavalry, operating against the hostile Sioux. He filled every position, and met every emergency with so much bravery, competence and intelligence as to command the general admiration and respect of the officers, and become chief of Scouts of the Department. All his successes have been conducted on the most honorable principles.

W. B. ROYALL, Colonel 4th Cavalry, U. S. A.

HEADQUARTERS 1ST CAVALRY, FORT CUSTER, M. T.

I often recall your valuable services to the Government, as well as to myself, in years long gone by, specially during the Sioux difficulties, when you were attached to my command as Chief of Scouts. Your indomitable perseverance, incomprehensible instinct in discovering the trails of the Indians, particularly at night, no matter how dark or stormy, your physical powers of endurance in following the enemy until overtaken, and your unflinching courage, as exhibited on all occasions, won not only my own esteem and admiration, but that of the whole command. With my best wishes for your success, I remain your old friend,

N. A. M. DUDLEY, Colonel 1st Cavalry, Brevet Brigadier-General, U. S. A

TALLAHASSEE, FLA., January 12, 1887.

HON. WILLIAM F. CODY:—I take great pleasure in recommending you to the public, as a man who has a high reputation in the army as a Scout. No one has ever shown more bravery on the Western plains than yourself. I wish you success in your proposed visit to Great Britain. Your obedient servant,

JNO. H. KING, Brevet Major-General U. S. A.

"SPRING THAWS REVEAL BAD GUIDING."—*Dodge.*

LASSOING WILD HORSES ON THE PLATTE IN OLD DAYS.

LINES INSPIRED ON WITNESSING THE PRAIRIE CHIEF CARESSING HIS BABY DAUGHTER, LITTLE IRMA CODY

Only a baby's fingers patting a brawny cheek,
Only a laughing dimple in the chin so soft and sleek,
Only a cooing babble, only a frightened tear,
But it makes a man both brave and kind
To have them ever near.
The hand that seemed harsh and cruel,
Nerved by a righteous hate
As it cleft the heart of the Yellow Hand,
In revenge of Custer's fate,
Has the tender touch of a woman,
As, rifle and knife laid by,
He coos and tosses the baby,
Darling "apple of his eye."

—*Richmond.*

"BUFFALO BILL'S" HOME AND HORSE RANCH ON THE OLD FIGHTING GROUND OF THE PAWNEE AND SIOUX.

MR. NATE SALSBURY, DIRECTOR.

Born 1846, February 28th, in Freeport, Ill., the family being descendants of the early Vermont settlers, went out with the first Illinois troops; served through the entire Rebellion; was the youngest enlisted soldier in the Army of the Cumberland; wounded three times; is a member of Post 11, G. A. R., Department of Massachusetts; went on the stage in 1868; has acted before every English-speaking public in the world.

The Amusement Department will be under the personal supervision of this eminent actor, whose successful career is now a matter of American Stage History. Years of continued success as a caterer to the amusement loving public of this country, Australia, India and Europe, both as actor and manager, is a guarantee that the "Wild West" will be presented in a manner and style commensurate with his well-known managerial ability, and artistic judgment. MR. SALSBURY long ago invested heavily in the cattle business in Montana, and is now part owner of one of the largest and most valuable ranches in the Northwest. During his repeated visits to the same he became impressed with the scenes and episodes witnessed, and thought of the feasibility of presenting them as far as practicable to the citizens of the East. An interchange of opinions with COL. CODY disclosed a similar intention, so that to the fertile brains of MESSRS. CODY and SALSBURY we are indebted for the first conjuring up of this novel project. They spoke of it years ago, and SALSBURY went to Europe to see if it would be advisable to take such a show on the Continent. Meanwhile, with MR. SALSBURY's knowledge, "BUFFALO BILL" started the enterprise to see if it could be made successful in this country. Last year's experiences were proof that it could, and now all hands will join in getting up a "Wild West" show that will be remarkable in all respects.

"THE COW-BOY KID"—THE BOY MARKSMAN.

Johnnie Baker was born at O'Fallon's Bluffs, on the banks of the South Platte River, in Western Nebraska, in the year 1870. His father is the well-known "Old Lew Baker, the ranchman," and was the owner of Lew Baker's O'Fallon's Bluff Ranch, in its day an important landmark. This place was one of the most noted on the great overland trail—the scenes, incidents, Indian attacks, etc, belonging to exhaustive pages in the early history of that, in old times, exposed and dangerous section. Here Johnnie's babyhood was passed in unconscious proximity to dangers seldom courted by the most sturdy, and his first "bug-a-boo" was not of the maternal imagining, but an existing fact, continually threatening, in the shape of the heartless savage Sioux. Cradled amid such pioneer surroundings, and dandled on the knees of all the most celebrated frontiersmen, the genuine old buckskin trappers—the first frontier invaders—his childhood witnessed the declining glories of the buffalo-hunters' paradise (it being the heart of their domain), and the advent of his superior, "the long horn of Texas," and his necessary companion, "The Cow-Boy."

The appearance of these brave, generous, free-hearted, self-sacrificing rough riders of the plains, literally living in the saddle, enduring exposure, hunger, risk of health and life as a duty to the employer, gave him his first communion with society beyond the sod cabin threshold, and impressed his mind, as well as directed his aspirations, to an emulation of the manly qualities necessary to be ranked a true American Cowboy.

When the Pony Express, the Stage Coach, and the wagon-trains were supplanted by the steam-horse, Baker's station became useless, and "Old Lew" removed bag and baggage to North Platte, a little town of magical railroad growth. Here he built a fine house, which became the headquarters of the "old timers," and many a tenderfoot can remember the thrilling incidents related of "life on the trail"—a life that now belongs alone to history and to romance—while Old Lew dispensed hospitality like a prince. But the ways of "city life," a too big heart, of which the "shiftless, genial affinities" and rounders took due advantage, caused his former prosperity to be a remembrance only, and Johnnie to work manfully, for one of his age, to lend a helping hand. Perfectly at home in the saddle, he was never content unless with some cowboy outfit, or at MR. CODY'S (whose homestead, extensive horse and cattle ranches, are near), where his active spirit found congenial associations, until he became recognized as "BUFFALO BILL'S boy." In the winter months he occasionally went to school, and being an apt scholar, has a fair education.

MR. CODY, on organizing his distinctly American exhibition, could not leave little Johnnie out. He can be seen every day with the Wild West, mounted on his fiery little mustang, riding, roping, shooting—repeating on the mimic scene his own experience, and the boyhood life of his elder, more famed associates, and any boy of his own age who can excel him in shooting, riding, and lassoing can "break every man in the outfit," as there are none who will not risk their pile on "THE COW-BOY KID."

ANNIE OAKLEY—

(LITTLE SURE SHOT.)

This celebrated Girl Shot was born at Woodland, Ohio. Ever since a toddling child she has had an inherent love for fire-arms and hunting, and at the age of ten, she as often as ammunition was obtainable, would smuggle her brother's musket and steal into the woods where game at that time was plentiful. Naturally, she was a good shot, and came home well supplied with game. At the age of twelve she was presented with a light muzzle-loading shot gun, and also a breech-loading rifle. With the shot gun she improved rapidly, and became such a fine shot that she rarely missed a quail or pheasant, and, at the age of fourteen she had paid off a mortgage on her mother's homestead with money earned from the game and skins shot and trapped by herself alone—while her aim with rifle was so true that she was debarred from entering in the turkey matches which were the popular holiday amusement in that part of the country.

Then came a local reputation; and with improved fire-arms she attracted wider attention, and for the past several years she has been shooting before the public with great success, and, although she has many times beaten all records, like the modest little girl she is, she never uses the word Champion in connection with her name. "SITTING BULL," the great Indian Chief, after seeing her shoot in St. Paul, Minn., adopted her into the Sioux tribe, giving her the name of "WATANYA CICILLA," or, "LITTLE SURE SHOT."

The first two years before the public she devoted to Rifle and Pistol Shooting, and there is very little in that line she has not accomplished. At Tiffin, Ohio, she once shot a ten-cent piece held between the thumb and forefinger of an attendant at a distance of 30 feet. In April, 1884, she attempted to beat the best record made at balls thrown in the air—the best record was 984 made by Dr. Ruth. MISS OAKLEY used a Stevens' 22 cal. rifle and broke 943. In February, 1885, she attempted the feat of shooting 5,000 balls in one day, loading the guns herself. In this feat she used three 16-gauge hammer guns; the balls were thrown from three traps 15 yards rise; out of the 5,000 shot at, she broke 4,772; on the second thousand she only missed 16, making *the best* 1,000 ball record, 984. Besides the thousands of exhibitions she has given in Europe and America, she has shot in over 50 matches and tournaments, winning forty-one prizes; her collection of medals and fire-arms, all of which have been won or presented to her, is considered one of the finest in the world.

MISS OAKLEY is also an accomplished equestrienne, and her success with the public has been greatly enhanced by the fact that in dress, style, and execution she is as *original* as she is attractive.

THE RIFLE AS AN AID TO CIVILIZATION.

There is a trite saying that "the pen is mightier than the sword." It is an equally true one that the bullet is the pioneer of civilization, for it has gone hand in hand with the axe that cleared the forest, and with the family Bible and school book. Deadly as has been its mission in one sense, it has been merciful in another; for without the rifle ball we of America would not be to-day in the possession of a free and united country, and mighty in our strength.

And so has it been in the history of all people, from the time when David slew Goliath, down through the long line of ages, until in modern times, science has substituted for the stone from David's sling the terrible missiles that now decide the fate of nations. It is not therefore, so harsh an expression as it seems to be at first sight, that it is indeed the bullet which has been the forerunner of growth and development.

It is in the far West of America, however, and along our frontier, that the rifle has found its greatest use and become a part of the person and the household of the venturesome settler, the guide, the scout, and the soldier; for nowhere else in Christendom is it so much and so frequently a necessity for the preservation of life, and the defence of home and property. It is here, too, among the hunters on the plains and in the Rocky Mountains, that one sees the perfection of that skill in marksmanship that has become the wonder of those who are not accustomed to the daily use of weapons. Yet if it were not possessed—if there were not the quick eye, the sure aim, coolness in the moment of extreme danger, whether threatened by man or beast—life in that section would be of little value, and a man's home anything but a safe abiding place.

There are exceptional cases of men like "BUFFALO BILL," Major North, and others, whose names are more or less familiar among the mighty hunters of the West, who excel in the use of rifle and pistol, and to which, time and time again, they and those around them have owed their lives. And they are the worthy successors of a long line of marksmen whose names are also "familiar as household words." Who does not recall David Crockett and his death-dealing rifle in the Alamo? Daniel Boone, of Kentucky, and the heroic exploits that have been written concerning them in the early pages of our country's history?

It is to the end that the people of the East, or rather those who are not acquainted with the rough life of the border, and especially that portion of it in which the rifle plays so important a part, may personally witness some of the feats of Western men, that MESSRS. CODY & Co., have determined to introduce in their "great realistic pictures of Western life" a series of shooting exhibitions. The manner in which buffalo are hunted, the exciting chase at close quarters, the splendidly trained horses who participate in the chase, the hunt for elk, the stealthy devices of Indians in capturing the fleet-footed animals—all these will be illustrated in a manner that has never been witnessed East of the Mississippi River.—*Buell's Life on the Plains.*

A HISTORICAL COACH OF THE DEADWOOD LINE,

THE INDIANS' ATTACK ON WHICH WILL BE REPRESENTED IN "BUFFALO BILL'S" WILD WEST, AND ALSO ITS RESCUE BY THE SCOUTS AND PLAINSMEN.

The denizens of the Eastern States of the Union are accustomed to regard the West as the region of romance and adventure. And, in truth, its history abounds with thrilling incidents and surprising changes. Every inch of that beautiful country has been won from a cruel and savage foe by danger and conflict. In the terrible wars of the border which marked the early years of the Western settlements, the men signalized themselves by performing prodigies of valor, while the women, in their heroic courage and endurance, afforded a splendid example of devotion and self-sacrifice. The history of the wagon trains and stage coaches that preceded the railway is written all over with blood, and the story of suffering and disaster, often as it has been repeated, is only known in all of its horrid details to the bold frontiersmen who, as scouts and rangers, penetrated the strongholds of the Indians, and, backed by the gallant men of the army, became the *avant couriers* of Western civilization and the terror of the red man.

Among the most stirring episodes in the life of the Western pioneer are those connected with the opening of new lines of travel, for it is here, among the trails and canyons, where lurk the desperadoes of both races, that he is brought face to face with danger in its deadliest forms. No better illustration of this fact is furnished than in the history of the famous DEADWOOD COACH, the scarred and weather-beaten veteran of the original "star route" line of stages, established at a time when it was worth a man's life to sit on its box and journey from one end of its destination to the other. The accompanying picture affords an idea of the old relic, and it is because of its many associations with his own life that it has been purchased by "BUFFALO BILL," and added to the attractions of his "GREAT REALISTIC EXHIBITION OF WESTERN NOVELTIES."

It will be observed that it is a heavily built Concord stage, and is intended for a team of six horses. The body is swung on a pair of heavy leather underbraces, and has the usual thick "perches," "jacks," and brakes belonging to such a vehicle. It has a large leather "boot"—

behind, and another at the driver's foot-board. The coach was intended to seat twenty-one men —the driver and two men beside him, twelve inside, and the other six on top. As it now stands, the leather blinds of the windows are worn, the paint is faded, and it has a battered and travel-stained aspect that tells the story of hardship and adventure. Its trips began in 1875, when the owners were Messrs. Gilmour, Salsbury & Co. Luke Voorhees is the present manager. The route was between Cheyenne and Deadwood, *via* Fort Laramie, Rawhide Buttes, Hat or War Bonnet Creek, the place where "BUFFALO BILL" killed the Indian Chief, "Yellow Hand," on July 17, 1876, Cheyenne River, Red Canyon, and Custer. Owing to the long distance and dangers, the drivers were always chosen for their coolness, courage and skill.

In its first season the dangerous places on the route were Buffalo Gap, Lame Johnny Creek, Red Canyon, and Squaw Gap, all of which were made famous by scenes of slaughter and the deviltry of the banditti. Conspicuous among the latter were "Curley" Grimes, who was killed at Hogan's Ranch; "Peg-Legged" Bradley; Bill Price, who was killed on the Cheyenne River; "Dunk" Blackburn, who is now in the Nebraska State Prison, and others of the same class, representing the most fearless of the road agents of the West.

On the occasion of the first attack the driver, John Slaughter, a son of the present marshal of Cheyenne, was shot to pieces with buckshot. He fell to the ground, and the team ran away, escaping with the passengers and mail, and safely reached Greeley's Station. This occurred at White Wood Canyon. Slaughter's body was recovered, brought to Deadwood, and thence carried to Cheyenne, where it is now buried. The old coach here received its "baptism of fire," and during the ensuing summer passed through a variety of similar experiences, being frequently attacked. One of the most terrific of these raids was made by the Sioux Indians, but the assault was successfully repelled, although the two leading horses were killed. Several commercial travelers next suffered from a successful ambush, on which occasion a Mr. Liebman, of Chicago, was killed, and his companion shot through the shoulder.

After this stormy period it was fitted up as a treasure coach, and naturally became an object of renewed interest to the robbers; but owing to the strong force of what is known as "shotgun messengers" who accompanied the coach, it was a long time before the bandits succeeded in accomplishing their purpose. Among the most prominent of these messengers were Scott Davis, a splendid scout, and one of the self-appointed undertakers of many of the lawless characters of the neighborhood; Boone May, one of the best pistol shots in the Rocky Mountain regions, who killed Bill Price in the streets of Deadwood, together with "Curley" Grimes, one of the road agents; Jim May, a worthy brother—a twin in courage if not in birth. Few men have had more desperate encounters than he, and the transgressors of the law have had many an occasion to feel the results of his keen eye and strong arm whenever it has become necessary to face men who are prepared to "die with their boots on." Still another of these border heroes (for such they may be justly termed) is Gail Hill, now the deputy sheriff of Deadwood, and his frequent companion was Jesse Brown, an old-time Indian fighter, who has a record of incident and adventure that would make a book. These men constituted a sextette of as brave fellows as could be found on the frontier, and their names are all well known in that country.

At last, however, some of them came to grief. The bandits themselves were old fighters. The shrewdness of one party was offset by that of the other, and on an unlucky day the celebrated Cold Spring tragedy occurred. The station had been captured, and the road agents secretly occupied the place. The stage arrived in its usual manner, and without suspicion of danger the driver, Gene Barnett, halted at the stable door. An instant afterward a volley was delivered that killed Hughey Stevenson, sent the buckshot through the body of Gail Hill, and dangerously wounded two others of the guards. The bandits then captured the outfit, amounting to some sixty thousand dollars in gold.

On another occasion the coach was attacked, and, when the driver was killed, saved by a woman—Martha Canary, better known at the present time in the wild history of the frontier as "Calamity Jane." Amid the fire of the attack, she seized the lines, and, whipping up the team, safely brought the coach to her destination.

When "BUFFALO BILL" returned from his scout with Gen. Crook, in 1876, he rode in this self-same stage, bringing with him the scalps of several of the Indians whom he had met. When afterward he learned that it had been attacked and abandoned, and was lying neglected on the plains, he organized a party, and, starting on the trail, rescued and brought the vehicle into camp.

With the sentiment that attaches to a man whose life has been identified with the excitement of the Far West, the scout has now secured the coach from Col. Voorhees, the manager of the Black Hills stage line, and hereafter it will play a differert role in its history from that of inviting murder and being the tomb of its passengers. And yet the "Deadwood Coach" will play no small part in the entertainment that has been organized by "BUFFALO BILL" and partner for the purpose of representing some of the most startling realities of Western life, in a vivid representation of one of the Indian and road agents' combined attacks.

THE COW-BOYS.

Among the many features of the Wild West not the least attractive will be the advent in the East of a band of veritable "cow-boys," a class without whose aid the great grazing pampas of the West would be valueless, and the Eastern necessities of the table, the tan-yard, and the factory would be meager. These will be the genuine cattle-herders of a reputable trade, and not the later misnomers of "the road," who, in assuming an honored title, have tarnished it in the East, while being in fact the cow-boys' greatest foe, the thieving, criminal "rustler." To *Wilkes' Spirit* of March, the editor is indebted for a just tribute and description of the American ranchman:—

"THE COW-BOY.—The cowboy! How often spoken of, how falsely imagined, how greatly despised (where not known), how little understood! I've been there considerable. How sneeringly referred to, and how little appreciated, although his title has been gained by the possession of many of the noblest qualities that form the romantic hero of the poet, novelist, and historian; the plainsman and the scout. What a school it has been for the latter! As 'tall oaks from little acorns grow,' the cow-boy serves a purpose, and often develops into the most celebrated ranchman, guide, cattle-king, Indian-fighter, and dashing ranger. How old Sam Houston loved them, how the Mexicans hated them, how Davy Crockett admired them, how the Comanches feared them, and how much you 'beef-eaters' of the rest of the country owe to them, is a large-sized conundrum. Composed of many 'to the manner born,' but recruited largely from Eastern young men they were taught at school to admire the deceased little George, in exploring adventares, and, though not equaling him in the 'cherry-tree goodness,' were more disposed to kick against the bull-dozing of teachers, parents, and guardians.

"As the rebellious kid of old times filled a handkerchief (always a handkerchief, I believe) with his all, and followed the trail of his idol, Columbus, and became a sailor bold, the more ambitious and adventurous youngster of later days freezes on to a double-barreled pistol and steers for the bald prairie to seek fortune and experience. If he don't get his system full it's only because the young man weakens, takes a back seat, or fails to become a Texas cow-boy. If his Sunday school ma'am has not impressed him thoroughly with the chapter about our friend Job, he may at first be astonished, but he'll soon learn the patience of the old hero, and think he pegged out a little too soon to take it all in. As there are generally openings, likely young fellows can enter, and not fail to be put through. If he is a stayer, youth and size will be no disadvantage for his start in, as certain lines of the business are peculiarly adapted to the light young horsemen, and such are highly esteemed when they become thoroughbreds, and fully possessed of 'cow sense.'

"Now 'cow sense' in Texas implies a thorough knowledge of the business, and a natural instinct to divine every thought, trick, intention, want, habit, or desire of his drove, under any and all circumstances. A man might be brought up in the States swinging to a cow's tail, yet, taken to Texas, would be as useless as a last year's bird's nest with the bottom punched out

The boys grow old soon, and the old cattle-men seem to grow young; thus it is that the name is applied to all who follow the trade. The boys are divided into range-workers and branders, road drivers and herders, trail-guides and bosses.

"As the railroads have now put an end to the old-time trips, I will have to go back a few years to give a proper estimate of the duties and dangers, delights and joys, trials and troubles, when off the ranch. The ranch itself and the cattle trade in the State still flourish in their old-time glory, but are being slowly encroached upon by the modern improvements that will, in course of time, wipe out the necessity of his day, the typical subject of my sketch. Before being counted in and fully indorsed, the candidate has had to become an expert horseman, and test the many eccentricities of the stubborn mustang; enjoy the beauties, learn to catch, throw, fondle—oh! yes, gently fondle (but not from behind)—and ride the 'docile' little Spanish-American plug, an amusing experience in itself, in which you are taught all the mysteries of rear and tear, stop and drop, lay and roll, kick and bite, on and off, under and over, heads and tails, hand springs, triple somersaults, standing on your head, diving, flip flaps, getting left (horse leaving you fifteen miles from camp—Indians in the neighborhood, etc.), and all the funny business included in the familiar term of 'bucking;' then learn to handle a rope, catch a calf, stop a crazy cow, throw a beef steer, play with a wild bull, lasso an untamed mustang, and daily endure the dangers of a Spanish matador, with a little Indian scrape thrown in, and if there is anything left of you they'll christen it a first-class cow-boy. Now his troubles begin (I have been worn to a frizzled end many times before I began); but after this he will learn to enjoy them—after they are over.

"As the general trade on the range has often been described, I'll simply refer to a few incidents of a trip over the plains to the cattle markets of the North, through the wild and unsettled portions of the Territories, varying in distance from fifteen hundred to two thousand miles—time, three to six months—extending through the Indian Territory and Kansas to Nebraska, Colorado, Dakota, Montana, Idaho, Nevada and sometimes as far as California. Immense herds, as high as thirty thousand or more in number, are moved by single owners, but are driven in bands of from one to three thousand, which, when under way, are designated 'herds.' Each of these has from ten to fifteen men, with a wagon driver and cook, and the 'kingpin of the outfit,' the boss, with a supply of two or three ponies to a man, an ox team, and blankets; also jerked beef and corn meal—the staple food. They are also furnished with mavericks or 'doubtless-owned' yearlings for the fresh meat supply. After getting fully under way, and the cattle broke in, from ten to fifteen miles a day is the average, and everything is plain sailing in fair weather. As night comes on, the cattle are rounded up in a small compass, and held until they lie down, when two men are left on watch, riding round and round them in opposite directions, singing or whistling all the time, for two hours, that being the length of each watch. The singing is absolutely necessary, as it seems to soothe the fears of the cattle, scares away the wolves or other varmints that may be prowling around, and prevents them from hearing any other accidental sound, or dreaming of their old homes, and if stopped would, in all probability, be the signal for a general stampede. 'Music hath charms to soothe the savage breast,' if a cow-boy's compulsory bawling out lines of his own composition :

Lay nicely now, cattle, don't heed any rattle,
But quietly rest until morn ;
For if you skedaddle, we'll jump in the saddle,
And head you as sure as you're born.

can be considered such.

Some poet may yet make a hit
On the odds and ends of cow-boys' wit.

"But on nights when 'Old Prob' goes on a spree, leaves the bung out of his water-barrel above, prowls around with his flash-box, raising a breeze, whispering in tones of thunder, and the cow boy's voice, like the rest of the outfit, is drowned out, steer clear, and prepare for action. If them quadrupeds don't go insane, turn tail to the storm, and strike out for civil and religious liberty, then I don't know what 'strike out' means. Ordinarily so clumsy and stupid-looking, a thousand beef steers can rise like a flock of quail on the roof of an exploding powder mill, and will scud away like a tumble weed before a high wind, with a noise like a receding earthquake. Then comes fun and frollic for the boys!

"Talk of 'Sheridan's ride, twenty miles away!' That was in the daytime, but this is the cow-boy's ride with Texas five hundred miles away, and them steers steering straight for home ; night time, darker than the word means, hog wallows, prairie dog, wolf and badger holes, ravines and precipices ahead, and if you do your duty, three thousand stampeding steers behind. If your horse don't swap ends, and you hang to them until daylight, you can bless your lucky stars. Many have passed in their checks at this game. The remembrance of the few that were foot loose on the Bowery a few years ago will give an approximate idea of the three thousand raving bovines on the war path. As they tear through the storm at one flash of lightning, they look all tails, and at the next flash all horns If Napoleon had had a herd at Sedan, headed in the right direction, he would have driven old Billy across the Rhine.

"The next great trouble is in crossing streams, which are invariably high in the driving season. When cattle strike swimming water they generally try to turn back, which eventuates in their 'milling,' that is, swimming in a circle, and, if allowed to continue, would result in the drowning of many. There the daring herder must leave his pony, doff his togs, scramble over their backs and horns to scatter them, and with whoops and yells, splashing, dashing, and didoes in the water, scare them to the opposite bank. This is not always done in a moment, for a steer is no fool of a swimmer ; I have seen one hold his own for six hours in the Gulf after having jumped overboard. As some of the streams are very rapid, and a quarter to half-a mile wide, considerable drifting is done. Then the naked herder has plenty of amusement in the hot sun, fighting green-head flies and mosquitoes, and peeping around for Indians, until the rest of the lay-out is put over—not an easy job. A temporary boat has to be made of the wagon-box, by tacking the canvas cover over the bottom, with which the ammunition and grub is ferried across, and the running-gear and ponies are swum over afterward. Indian fights and horse thief troubles are part of the regular rations. Mixing with other herds and cutting them out, again avoiding too much water at times, and hunting for a drop at others, belongs to the regular routine.

"Buffalo chips for wood a great portion of the way (poor substitute in wet weather) and the avoiding of prairie fires later on, vary the monotony. In fact, it would fill a book to give a detailed account of a single trip, and it is no wonder the boys are hilarious when it ends, and, like the old toper, 'swears no more for me,' only to return and go through the mill again.

"How many, though, never finish, but mark the trail with their silent graves ! no one can tell. But when Gabriel toots his horn, the 'Chisholm trail' will swarm with cow-boys. 'Howsomever, we'll all be thar,' let's hope for a happy trip, when we say to this planet, *adios !*

J. B. OMOHUNDRO (TEXAS JACK)."

THE VAQUERO OF THE SOUTHWEST.

Between the "cow-boy" and the "vaquero" there is only a slight line of demarcation. The one is usually an American, inured from boyhood to the excitements and hardships of his life, and the other represents in his blood the stock of the Mexican, or it may be of the half-breed.

In their work, the methods of the two are similar ; and, to a certain extent, the same is true of their associations. Your genuine vaquero, however, is generally, when off duty, more of a dandy in the style and get-up of his attire than his careless and impetuous compeer. He is fond of gaudy clothes, and when you see him riding well mounted into a frontier town, the first thought of an Eastern man is, that a circus has broken loose in the neighborhood, and this is one of the performers. The familiar broad-rimmed sombrero covers his head; a rich jacket, embroidered by his sweetheart perhaps, envelopes his shapely shoulders ; a sash of blue or red silk is wrapped around his waist, from which protrude a pair of revolvers ; and buckskin trousers, slit from the knee to the foot, and ornamented with rows of brass or silver buttons, complete his attire, save that enormous spurs, with jingling pendants, are fastened to the boots, and announce in no uncertain sound the presence of the *beau ideal* vaquero in full dress.

His saddle is of the pure Mexican type, with high pommel, whereon hangs the inevitable lariat, which in his hands is almost as certain as a rifle shot.

Ordinarily he is a peaceful young fellow, but when the whisky is present in undue proportions, he is a good individual to avoid. Like the cow-boy, he is brave, nimble, careless of his own life, and reckless, when occasion requires, of those of other people. At heart he is not bad. The dependence on himself which his calling demands, the dangers to which he is subjected while on duty, all compel a sturdy self-reliance, and he is not slow in exhibiting the fact that he possesses it in a sufficient degree at least for his own protection. True types of this peculiar class, seen nowhere else than on the plains, will be among the attractions of the show ; and the men will illustrate the methods of their lives in connection with the pursuit and catching of animals, together with the superb horsemanship that is characteristic of their training.

ON A MUSTANG.

By the Editor of "Texas Siftings."

The majority of Texas ponies buck, or pitch, as it is sometimes termed, whenever circumstances seem to demand an exhibition of this facetious break, or the condition of things seems to justify the sportive caprice. In fact, some ponies will buck for hours, only stopping to get breath for a fresh start. This kind is recommended for the use of dyspeptics and invalids suffering from torpidity of liver. A pitching mustang, when working on full time and strictly devoting his attention to business, is the most moving sight I ever beheld. His spine seems to be of whalebone, and he appears to possess all the elements of a steamboat explosion, a high-pressure pile-driver, an earthquake, in addition to the enthusiasm of a county convention. We were glad to find that ours were not bucking ponies, and we congratulated each other on the fortunate circumstance. Of course, as we argued, if there had been any buck in them it would have developed itself at an early stage in the journey. Understand, we were not afraid. I named my pony "Deliberation;" the name seemed so appropriate—no pomp or circumstance about him—and he was so gentle and tranquil ; nothing seemed to flurry him. You could throw the reins on his neck and strike a match on the pommel of the saddle. I say you *could* do this, but the after fate of that match would be of no moment to you ; you would be other-

wise engaged. I regret to say that I tried the experiment. I lighted a match—at least I think I did —but there was a haziness about the subsequent proceedings that prevents accuracy of statement. I distinctly remember striking the match. At that moment, however, I was fluently propelled upward; a tornado caught me—whirled me around eleven times. As I came down a pile-driver drove me in the stomach, and I came to earth with that sensation (only intensified) that a man feels who sits down in what he imagines to be a high chair, and which he afterward thinks was about seven feet lower than his estimate. I saw whole milky ways of constellations that never before existed. I realized for the first time the dense solidity of the earth, and made the astonishing discovery that under certain circumstances our planet, instead of revolving on its own axis once in every twenty-four hours, can rush around at the rate of at least one hundred revolutions a minute. There is not in the whole range of languages, ancient, modern, or profane, terms sufficiently expressive to describe the state of my feelings, the amount of mud on my person, or the chaotic condition of my brain. As soon as the earth settled down to the usual speed of her diurnal motion, I came to the conclusion that it was not always best to judge by appearances. I had been hasty in bestowing a distinctive cognomen on my erratic steed. He had no more deliberation in him than has a fugitive flea under the searching scrutiny of a determined woman. I re-named him. This time I called him "Delay," because delay is—but it does not matter.

Come to think of it since, the reason was weak. If, however, the reader should pierce the intricate labyrinth of mental ingenuity that constitutes the conundrum, I trust he will be charitable enough to consider the circumstances connected with its perpetration.

There are times that try men's souls. There are seasons in every Christian's life when he wishes he was not a church member for just about five minutes, that he might have a chance to do justice to the surroundings. Such to me was the trying moment when I gathered my bruised remains together, and, looking around, saw the festive "Delay" quietly eating grass, while a little distance off sat the doctor on his pony, complacently whistling, "Earth hath no sorrow that Heaven cannot heal."

GENERAL-CONSULATE OF THE UNITED STATES OF AMERICA.

MR. NATE SALSBURY. ROME, 3D MARCH, 1890.

RESPECTED SIR:—

The Roman papers report that COLONEL CODY has engaged with Don Onorio Caetani Herzogs of Sermoneta, Prince of Teano, etc., etc., that he will to-morrow ride in the Exhibition of this town some of his untamed stallions.

I send you, therefore, some of this gentleman's reference lists, also information as to his family and his horses, which may be of interest at this time.

The great lordly family of the Cajetans is the oldest amongst the noble families of Rome. The Cajetans were once the lords over the entire Roman districts of Velletri (twenty-five miles south of Rome), near Fondi (on the Terracina side).

They gave two Pontiffs to the Throne of St. Peter, Gelasius II. (1118), and Boniface VII. (1294), and were the close allies of the Colonnas and the Orsinis, in their long contests with the Papacy in the eleventh and twelfth centuries.

Their large estates were confiscated by Pope Alexander VI. (1492–1503), but were afterward restored under another Pontiff.

The present chief representative of the family is Don Onorio Caetani Herzog of Sermoneta, Prince of Teano, etc., etc. He is the son of the late Prince Michael Angelo Caetani, renowned for his studies and commentaries on the works of the poet Dante and his manifold services in the interests of Italian culture and art in general.

The family residence in Rome is the Cajetan Palace, where the family pedigree and archives are kept.

These genealogies and documents are the most complete of all the great historic Roman families. Some of the branches of the pedigree are dated back into Cajetans of the ninth and tenth centuries.

The small village of Cisterna, where the untamed stallions are kept, lies about thirty-one miles south of Rome; it is situated on the same line as the old Appian Way. The archæological and historic name of the village was "The Three Taverns," where the holy Apostle Paul (in the Book of Acts, chapter xviii. and 15th verse) arrived, and found some of his friends come to meet him, on his journey toward Rome.

This ancient site, and the whole surrounding district, is still the property of the Cajetans.

The Prince's horses, which will be chosen for this test from the Cisterna Campagna, are known in Rome as the Cajetan breed, and hold their own for the wildest and most unmanageable in the country.

It is said that this breed shows a local crossing with a Saracen breed (which was introduced into these parts by the Saracens in the Middle Ages), and also a touch of English full blood.

Whole volumes of illustrious history might be supplied with reference to the Cajetan family and of their richly endowed estate; they have filled a spacious position in the annals of a thousand years. With sincere respect, (Signed), CHARLES M. WOOD,

Vice-Consul of the United States of America at Rome, Italy.

ROMAN WILD HORSES.

TAMED BY COW-BOYS. RIDDEN IN FIVE MINUTES. HOW "BUFFALO BILL'S" COW-BOYS TAME THE ROMAN WILD HORSES.

(Per the Commercial Cable to the "Herald.") ROME, 4TH MARCH, 1890.

All Rome was to-day astir over an attempt of "BUFFALO BILL'S" cow-boys with wild horses, which were provided for the occasion by the Prince of Sermoneta.

Several days past the Roman authorities have been busy with the erection of specially-cut barriers for the purpose of keeping back the wild horses from the crowds.

The animals are from the celebrated stud of the Prince of Sermoneta, and the Prince himself declared that no cow-boy in the world could ride these horses. The cow-boys laughed over this surmise, and then offered at least to undertake to mount one of them, if they might choose it.

Every man, woman, and child expected that two or three people would be killed by this attempt.

The anxiety and enthusiasm was great. Over 2,000 carriages were ranged round the field, and more than 20,000 people lined the spacious barriers. Lord Dufferin and many other Diplomatists were on the Terrace, and amongst Romans were presently seen the consort of the Prime Minister Crispi, the Prince of Torlonia, Madame Depretis, Princess Colonna, Gravina Antonelli, the Baroness Reugis, Princess Brancaccia, Grave Giannotti, and critics from amongst the highest aristocracy. In five minutes the horses were tamed.

Two of the wild horses were driven without saddle or bridle in the Arena. "BUFFALO BILL" gave out that they would be tamed. The brutes made springs into the air, darted hither and thither in all directions, and bent themselves into all sorts of shapes, but all in vain.

In five minutes the cow-boys had caught the wild horses with the lasso, saddled, subdued, and bestrode them. Then the cow-boys rode them round the Arena, whilst the dense crowds of people applauded with delight.

"BUFFALO BILL" IN VENICE.

(By Telegraph, "New York Herald.") VENICE, 16TH APRIL, 1890.

"BUFFALO BILL" and his "Wild West" have made a big show in Venice. This evening the directors have a special invitation on the Grand Canal, where the whole troupe will be shown. COLONEL CODY is taken by the Venetian Prefect in his own private residence. No one can think them ordinary artists, after they have seen the gathering of different Indians in gondolas, or seen the wonderful sight which presents itself at the Venetian Palace, and in the little steamboats that ply between the Pier of St. Mark and the Ra lway Station.

Thousands of Venetians assembled yesterday at Verona, where the Company of the Municipal Authorities of Justice have allowed the use of the Amphitheatre, or the so-called Arena, one of the most interesting structures of Italy, and nearly so with the Colosseum of Rome itself.

45,000 persons can conveniently find sitting room in this Arena, and for standing room there is also extensive space. As His Royal Highness Victor Emanuel was on a visit here once, 60,000 people were accommodated in it. It is, perhaps, interesting to know that this building is the largest in the world, although the "Wild West" Show quite filled it.

The Amphitheatre (Arena) was built in the year 290 A. D., under Diocletian, and is known in Germany as the Home of the Dietrich of Bern. It is 106 feet high, 168 meters long, and 134 meters broad (the Arena itself is 83 meters long, 48 meters broad), the circumference is 525 meters. In the surrounding Amphitheatre (entering by the west side through Arch No. 5, admission one franc, Sunday free), are five-and-forty rows of steps, 18 inches high, 26 inches broad, built of grey, or rather reddish yellow limestone, where nearly 20,000 spectators can find places, and where many more people can see by standing on the wooden benches behind them. From an inscription on the second story, it will be remembered that Napoleon I. visited this place in 1805. The restoration of the building was by recommendation of that Emperor. A wonderful view is obtained from the higher steps.

THE WILD WEST AT THE VATICAN.—"BUFFALO BILL'S" INDIANS AND COW-BOYS AT THE ANNIVERSARY CEREMONY OF LEO XIII.

New York Herald, March, 4, 1890.—(From our Special Correspondent.) ROME, March 3.

One of the strangest spectacles ever seen within the venerable walls of the Vatican was the dramatic entry of "BUFFALO BILL" at the head of his Indians and cow-boys this morning when the ecclesiastical and secular military court of the Holy See assembled to witness the twelfth annual thanksgiving of Leo XIII, for his coronation. In the midst of the splendid scene, crowded with the old Roman aristocracy, and surrounded by walls immortalized by Michael Angelo and Rafael, there suddenly appeared a host of savages in war paint, feathers and blankets, carrying tomahawks and knives.

A vast multitude surged in the great square before St. Peter's early in the morning to witness the arrival of the Americans. Before half-past nine o'clock the Ducal Hall, Royal Hall, and Sextine Chapel of the Vatican were packed with those who had influence enough to obtain admittance. Through the middle of the three audiences, the pathway was bordered with the brilliant uniforms of the Swiss Guards, Palatine Guards, Papal gendarmes and private chamberlains. The sunlight fell upon lines of glittering steel, nodding plumes, golden chains, shimmering robes of silk, and all the blazing emblems of pontifical power and glory.

THE WILD WEST MAKE THEIR ENTREE.

Suddenly, a tall and chivalrous figure appeared at the entrance, and all eyes were turned toward him. It was COLONEL W. F. CODY, "BUFFALO BILL." With a sweep of his great sombrero, he saluted the chamberlains, and then strode between the guards with his partner, MR. NATE SALSBURY, by his side.

"ROCKY BEAR" led the Sioux warriors, who brought up the rear. They were painted in every color that Indian imagination could devise. Every man carried something with which to make big medicine in the presence of the great medicine man sent by the Great Spirit.

"ROCKY BEAR" rolled his eyes and folded his hands on his breast as he stepped on tiptoe through the glowing sea of color. His braves furtively eyed the halberds and two-handed swords of the Swiss Guards.

The Indians and cowboys were ranged in the south corners of the Ducal Hall. COLONEL CODY and MR. SALSBURY were escorted into the Sextine Chapel by chamberlains, where they were greeted by Miss Sherman, daughter of General Sherman. A Princess invited COLONEL CODY to a place in the tribune of the Roman nobles.

He stood facing the gorgeous Diplomatic Corps, surrounded by the Prince and Princess Borghesi, the Marquis Serlupi, Princess Bandini, Duchess di Grazioli, Prince and Princess Massimo, Prince and Princess Ruspoli, and all the ancient noble families of the city.

THE PAPAL BLESSING.

When the Pope appeared in the *sedia gestatoria*, carried above the heads of his guards, preceded by the Knights of Malta and a procession of cardinals and archbishops, the cowboys bowed and so did the Indians. "ROCKY BEAR" knelt and made the sign of cross. The Pontiff leaned affectionately toward the rude groups and blessed them. He seemed to be touched by the sight.

As the Papal train swept on, the Indians became excited, and a squaw fainted. They had been warned not to utter a sound, and were with difficulty restrained from whooping. The Pope looked at COLONEL CODY intently as he passed, and the great scout and Indian fighter bent low as he received the Pontifical benediction.

After the Thanksgiving Mass, with its grand choral accompaniment and now and then the sound of Leo XIII's voice, heard ringing through the chapel, the great audience poured out of the Vatican.

A GREAT PONY-EXPRESS RIDE.

While riding Pony-Express between Red Buttes and Three Crossings, seventy-six miles, CODY had a dangerous and lonely route, including crossing of the North Platte river, one-half mile wide, often much swollen and turbulent. An average of fifteen miles an hour had to be made, including changes of horses, detours for safety, and time for meals.

On reaching Three Crossings, finding the rider on the next division, a route of eighty-six miles, had been killed during the night before, he made the extra trip on time. This round trip of three hundred and twenty-four miles, was made without a stop, except for meals and change of horses, one of the longest and best-ridden pony-express journeys ever made.—*Bull's History of the Plains.*

"OLD CHARLIE"—DIED AT SEA, 1888.

AMERICAN WILD WEST EXHIBITION.

Editorial from the London "Times," Nov. 1, 1887.—The American Exhibition, which has attracted all the town to West Brompton for the last few months, was brought yesterday to an appropriate and dignified close. A meeting of representative Englishmen and Americans was held, under the presidency of Lord Lorne, in support of the movement for establishing a Court of Arbitration for the settlement of disputes between this country and the United States. At first sight it might seem to be a far cry from the Wild West to an International Court. Yet the connection is not really very remote. Exhibitions of American products and scenes from the wilder phases of American life certainly tend in some degree at least to bring America nearer to England. They are partly cause and partly effect. They are the effect of increased and increasing intercourse between the two countries, and they tend to promote a still more intimate understanding. The two things, the Exhibition and the Wild West Show, supplemented each other. Those who went to be amused often staid to be instructed. The Wild West was irresistible. COLONEL CODY suddenly found himself the hero of the London season. Notwithstanding his daily engagements and his punctual fulfillment of them, he found time to go everywhere, to see everything, and to be seen by all the world. All London contributed to his triumph, and now the close of his show is selected as the occasion for promoting a great international movement with Mr. Bright, Lord Granville, Lord Wolseley and Lord Lorne for its sponsors. Civilization itself consents to march onward in the train of "BUFFALO BILL." COLONEL CODY can achieve no greater triumph than this, even if he some day realizes the design attributed to him of running the Wild West Show within the classic precincts of the Colosseum at Rome.

THE FIGHTING CHIEF, KICKING BEAR AND STAFF, CAMPAIGN 1891, PINE RIDGE.

This association of the cause of international arbitration with the fortunes of the American Wild West is not without its grotesque aspects. But it has a serious import, nevertheless. After all, the Americans and the English are one stock. Nothing that is American comes altogether amiss to an Englishman. We are apt to think that American life is not picturesque. We have been shown one of its most picturesque aspects. It is true that "RED SHIRT" would be as unusual a phenomenon in Broadway as in Cheapside. But the Wild West for all that is racy of the American soil. We can easily imagine Wall Street for ourselves; we need to be shown the Cowboys of Colorado. Hence it is no paradox to say that COLONEL CODY has done his part in bringing America and England nearer together.

"MAJOR" BURKE'S APPEAL FOR A PEACEFUL SOLUTION OF THE INDIAN TROUBLE.

[FROM "WASHINGTON POST."]

Perhaps one of the most eloquent and effective pleas for a peaceful solution of the Indian trouble was that made by MAJOR JOHN M. BURKE at the famous conference in the Ogalalla camp on the 17th of January, when negotiating for the Indians' surrender with Capt. Lee. The proceedings, as reported for the Department, gives Major Burke's remarks as follows:

"My friends, I came here on the invitation of many of my old Ogalalla friends who know me. I am happy to sit down among you to-day, because it is so much quieter than for some weeks. I do not come here in behalf of the Government or any society, but because I travel and live with the Indians, and they are my friends for many years. When I first heard of this trouble, GEN. CODY ('BUFFALO BILL') sent me to do what I could for you. I have been here eight or nine weeks—have listened, heard, and seen a great deal. From the first I saw no necessity for this trouble. A great deal of it came from a misunderstanding and the lack of confidence among the Indians as regards the intention of the Government. Our friend, Capt. Lee, does not carry arms, neither do I. While it looked like peace daily you were just like scared birds, ready to stampede at any time. I am going to Washington to see the great counsellors, and I want to be able to say that when I left all was peace, and that the Indians fully understood Gen. Miles' intention. I want you to place every confidence in him. When the earth loses something God sends something else, and when God took your friend Gen. Crook he sent you Gen. Miles, who is now your benefactor. The foundation of all good in men is truth and honor. When a man has these foundations he has right, and can stand open-handed and talk for his rights. He needs no gun, which is dangerous and causes trouble. You have thousands of friends in the East. Gen. Miles and Capt. Lee can reach those friends. I have this confidence there will be no war on the part of Gen. Miles, if you give up your arms, because through military discipline he can control his men, as soldiers have no interest to shoot Indians. Tell your young men to be calm and have confidence in Gen. Miles who will see you through. But you must discipline and control your young men. Let every man who talks mean what he says, and not talk to evade the question. I, to show you what confidence I have in Gen. Miles that he will not fire upon you and your women and children when you are disarmed, I will promise to live in your camp until you have confidence that the white chief will see no harm come to you. I am glad to hear that some chiefs are going to Washington, and hope instead of ten, twenty or twenty-five will go. I will be there to see you, and may go with you. I will do all I can in my humble way for you. Let us all work for peace between the white men and the red—not for a moment, a day, a year, but for ever, for eternity."

IMPROVED BY TRAVEL.—CHAMBERLAIN, S. D., DECEMBER 13.

The large number of Indians who have been abroad for the last few years with "BUFFALO BILL'S" Wild West show are doing some good work among the unruly Indians belonging to Rosebud and Pine Ridge agencies, and to their efforts as much as to any one thing can a prevention of an immediate outbreak among the red men be attributed. These Indians emphatically refused to listen to any proposition from the hostiles looking to their joining them, but have continued to act as peacemakers at all times since their return, and they are untiring in their efforts to bring about a peaceful settlement of the present difficulty. These Indians act in marked contrast to some of those educated, as many of the latter are among the hostiles.

MAJOR BURKE.—HE TALKS ON THE RECENT TROUBLES AT PINE RIDGE AGENCY.

MAJOR BURKE, tbe widely and favorably known business manager of "COLONEL CODY'S" Wild West aggregation, spent Sunday in the city, having just returned from Pine Ridge agency. The Major spent from the first day until after the surrender at the seat of the Indian war and did more than any other civilian at the Agency in the interest of peace and a speedy settlement of the trouble. Indeed, he was the central figure at Pine Ridge among the civilians, and even among the officials was a much deferred-to character of acknowledged power with the troubled children of the hills and plains.

"The *Bee's* dispatches have so fully and accurately reported the situation," said the major, "and they keep up so nearly to the last hour each day that I really have nothing new to say. The army and Indians now have a perfect respect for each other, and I think this will continue, for a time at least. The whole matter should I think, be left to General Miles and the appropriation committee of congress. I would not venture, as matters now stand, to predict how long we are to have this running peace. In fact, I scarcely think that any one feels like speaking for the future in the matter. As to the sending of chiefs to Washington, well that may and I hope will result advantageously. I have great faith in General Miles' judgment, and I think the president, the commissioner of Indian Affairs and congress will listen to them with much interest. We have had a very wild time at Pine Ridge, one of the most critical in all the history of Indian affairs, and with the whole country I fervently hope for a final settlement that will result in permanent peace."

MAJOR BURKE left last night for North Platte. He will return here on Tuesday, and on Wednesday leave for Washington. He has great cause for congratulation on the manner in which those Indians whom he has taken over Europe have conducted themselves during the trying scenes just passed. At all times they were found earnest and patient advocates of peace and obedience to law, as well as energetic scouts, police, peace commissioners and spies.—*Cressy*—War correspondent Omaha *Bee*.

"BUFFALO BILL" VICTORIOUS.—THE SIOUX AND WILD WEST SHOWS.

Editorial from "New York Sun," Tuesday, March 10th.

The permission granted by the Interior Department to "BUFFALO BILL" to engage 100 Indians for his "Wild West Show" is a great victory for Bill. It is a more conspicuous success even than that which he achieved during the recent Pine Ridge campaign, when, as a brigadier general commanding the Nebraska State forces, he received a written acknowledgment of his services from Gen. Miles. It has been accomplished, moreover, directly in the face of, for some unexplained reason, enormous obstacles which "BUFFALO BILL" found in his path; and the skill and success with which he surmounted them are proportionately great. First he brought his braves from Europe to Washington to show the refining and ennobling influence which European travel had had upon them. Then when the Sioux troubles broke out, and threatened to wreck his plans, especially as it was charged that the complaints of some of his troop had aggravated the tribal discontent, he found in that very disaster his opportunity, and hastening to the scene, took care that none of his recent performers should be conspicuously hostile to the Government, but enlisted many on the side of the Government, doing splendid service. His next step was to procure recommendations from army officers, showing Secretary Noble the military wisdom of allowing some of the young restless Sioux braves to be taken away from the reservation, under his charge. The issue was then between "BUFFALO BILL" and the Commissioner, and the former won.

To the eminent patrons of the Wild West Show this great victory will be very welcome. And now the best thing for the Commissioner and the defeated objectors to do is to accept the first chance to see the show. They will probably enjoy the spectacle, and be proud of the professional progress of their wards.

BUFFALO BILL'S INDIANS EXAMINED OFFICIALLY. —*From Lincoln (Neb.) Journal.*

Pine Ridge Agency, S. D., (via Rushville, Neb.) Dec. 3.—[Special.]—Nothing farther has transpired to effect a change at Pine Ridge at this writing. All is quiet, but few reports of any kind arriving, and the general routine of camp life is the only variation, if it may be so called, of the monotony of life. Long trains of supplies and ammunition have been daily coming in from Rushville to this place. If anything is to be judged by the preparations being made one would suppose the army officers expected a long and severe campaign.

Orders were received to-day by Agent Royer to examine "BUFFALO BILL'S" Indians, all of which are at this place, about fifty being on the police force and in the company of scouts sent to Lieutenant Taylor to Fort Robinson for duty there. All here were thoroughly examined by Agent Royer and Special Agent Cooper as to their pay, clothing, food and general welfare, and all spoke in the highest praise of MR. CODY and his treatment of them while abroad. Not one had a complaint of any character to make. This is a pretty effectual denial of the various charges lodged against "BUFFALO BILL" and his managers.—W. F. K.

MACAULAY'S NEW ZEALANDER.—THE LAST OF THE MOHICANS.—THE LAST OF THE BUFFALO.—

From Manchester Courier, April, 1888.

An addition which has just been made to the United States National Museum at Washington, affords important subsidiary evidence, if such were needed, of the unique interest attending the extraordinary exhibition at Manchester illustrative of the Wild West. Naturalists have not too soon become alive to the remarkable fact that those shaggy monarchs of the prairie, the ponderous buffalo tribe, are well nigh extinct. They have dwindled away before the exterminating tread of the hunter and the march of the pioneer of civilization. The prairie no longer shakes beneath the impetuous advance of the mighty herd, and even individual specimens are becoming scarce. The representatives of the Smithsonian Museum in America therefore sent out an expedition into the West in search of what buffaloes there might be remaining, in order that the country might preserve some memento of the millions of those animals, which not many years ago roamed over the prairies. Twenty-five animals in all were captured, six of which have been arranged in a group for exhibition. One of the American papers describes this as the transference of a little bit of Montana—a small square patch from the wildest part of the Wild West—to the National Museum. The idea is one which is exactly applicable to COLONEL W. F. CODY'S collection, which is approaching its last days of residence among us. Those scenes in which the primeval forest and the vast expanse of prairie are represented, with elk and bison careering about, chased by the hunter and the scout, is a transference from the Wild West which, as we now learn, should be even more interesting to the naturalist than it is to either the artistic or the historical student. We leave out of view for the moment the ordinary spectator who goes only to be amused or entertained, independently of any instruction that may be afforded. These scenes, moreover, are all the more interesting to the ethnological student because of the association with them of the red men who have been indigenous to the prairies and their surroundings. The occupation of Uncas, like Othello's, is gone; palatial buildings and busy streets have succeeded to the wigwam and the happy hunting grounds, and the successor of Fenimore Cooper may find his representative Indians, not where the hunting knife and tomahawk are needed, but in the arena of mimic battle and adventure. The Indian is going out with the buffalo; mayhap we shall ere long see the last of his descendants, with the contemplative gaze of Macaulay's New Zealander, sitting before the group in the Smithsonian Museum, looking upon the last representatives of the extinct buffalo, fixed in its prairie-like surroundings. These considerations of facts which force themselves upon the imagination, distinctly enhance the interest of those "pictures" from the Wild West, presented with such force and realism by the ruling genius, who, anent the purport of these reflections, is so appropriately named "BUFFALO BILL." In the course of a very short time these pictures will permanently vanish from English soil, as they are to be produced in America soon, and it may be expected that those in arrears in information respecting them, and who appreciate as they deserve to be appreciated, their instructive features, will give to them a concentrated attention ere it is too late.

EXPLICIT DENIAL OF THE VARIOUS CHARGES MADE AGAINST "BUFFALO BILL."

[By the Commercial Cable to the Herald.]

HERALD BUREAU, NO. 49, AVENUE DE L'OPERA, PARIS, July 24, 1890.

The Herald's European edition publishes to-day the following:

BERLIN, July 24, 1890.

TO THE EDITOR OF THE HERALD:—The statements and general inference in the *Herald* about starvation and cruelty in the Wild West camp are ridiculously untruthful, and unjust to CODY and SALSBURY. I appeal to your sense of justice to fully deny the same.

The Wild West is under the public eye daily, and in all the countries and cities visited, under rigid police and health inspection. Our cuisine is the same as in New York, Paris and London, and has challenged the admiration and astonishment of the citizens of every place visited for its quality and quantity. Our contracts and beef bills will bear witness as well as the United States Consuls and local officials, and thousands of others who have daily visited our camp.

Our pride as well as our interest, lies in the good food and good health of our people. As regards the steerage passage, the steamships don't want to give cabin passage to Indians. Many a good white man has gone across the ocean in the steerage. Would that every white man in the world was as well fed, clothed and looked after as our red tourists of "BUFFALO BILL'S" Wild West.

(Signed) JOHN M. BURKE.

NEW YORK HERALD. BERLIN, July 24.

We take great pleasure in stating that we visited the "BUFFALO BILL" Wild West Show in Berlin, and have seen the Indians both in their tents and during the performance.

They are certainly the best looking and apparently the best fed Indians we have ever seen.

(Signed) W. H. EDWARDS, *Consul General.*
(Signed) CHAS. H. JOHNSON, *U. S. Consul at Hamburg.*
(Signed) C. COLEMAN, *Sec. of Leg., Berlin.*

VALUE OF AN INTERNATIONAL JOURNAL DEMONSTRATED.

Telegram to Paris Edition from N. Y. Herald, July 25.

The friends of "BUFFALO BILL" are delighted with the authoritative denial of the charge of cruelty to his Indians, cabled to the *Herald* this morning. It shows the value of an international paper that stories wilder than the Wild West itself can be so promptly sat upon and refuted.

His accusers have not yet produced that statement bearing out his charges, and it looks now as if their good nature and charity had been buncoed by the wily White Horse.

CONSHOHOCKEN, PA., July 30, 1888. MESSRS. CODY & SALSBURY,—DEAR SIRS: Having had every opportunity for five consecutive days and nights to inspect the discipline, and to study the effect of the general influence of your exhibition upon the Indians with you, I wish, by this note, **to express my gratification with it all. I have seen the Indians learning promptness, regularity,** cleanliness in person and food, and also learning to do well the work for which they were employed. That anything in the shape of evil will not do, but must come up to a standard.

I saw them learning to realize that they were not hired merely to receive their pay, or, if possible, to "boss" the job, and have their own way about it. Knowing that the brothers of many of these men have offered to take care of their families, stock and farms, while these go away to earn money to help all, I can but class your great exhibition as an industry which will benefit the Indians of Pine Ridge Reservation. Most respectfully yours, JNO. ROBINSON,
Missionary Pine Ridge Agency, Dakota.

COL. T. A. DODGE, U. S. A., *re* U. S. CAVALRY.

Harper's Weekly, June, 1891.

This able magazine has done effective work in the past years in faithfully illustrating the same subject that the Wild West is simplifying to the present generation by animated tableaux —thus aiding the permanent character of the marvelously correct and imperishable illustrations of their artist, Fred Remington (and their contributors—notably Col. Dodge and Theo. Roosevelt), time enhancing the literary, artistic, and historical value of their work. Liberty has been taken to cull some information regarding the cavalry riders, with the addition by the compiler of last winter's remarkable Relief of Pine Ridge Ride, by Guy Henry's command, whose dark-skinned "Buffaloes" furnish a chapter to Western experience by having their feet "chilblained" and their thin faces sunburned (by old Sol's reflection from the snow) on the same day. Col. Dodge intelligently discourses on American riders, and relates the following cavalry trips:

"Our Western cavalry is now the pattern of the cavalry of the future. Let us quote some isolated facts, quite apart from the civil war, to show that our cavalrymen on Indian service have stout hearts under their army blue as well as stout seats in the saddle, and earn credit for them both. Mention need not be made of the risk every scouting party or detachment runs of perishing in an Indian ambush, like Custer or Forsyth; nor of frightful marches of many days with the thermometer at forty degrees below zero, like the command of Henry. Let us look at some good distance riding, for it is in this that our men excel. General Merritt, in 1879, rode with a battalion of the Fifth Cavalry to the relief of Payne, and covered one hundred and seventy miles from 11 A. M., October 2d, to 5:30 P. M., October 5th—two days and six hours—accompanied by a battalion of infantry in wagons, which much retarded the march. He arrived on the scene in good order, and ready for a fight. Single couriers had ridden in over the same distance from Thornburg's command during the previous two or three days in less than twenty-four hours. Captain F. S. Dodge marched his command on the same occasion eighty miles in sixteen hours. Lieutenant Wood, of the Fourth Cavalry, marched his troop seventy miles in twelve hours—6 A. M. to 6 P. M.—and came in fresh; and double that distance has been made from 10 A. M. to 5 P. M. next day. In 1870 four men of Company H, First Cavalry, bore dispatches from Fort Harney to Fort Warner, one hundred and forty miles, over a bad road—twenty of it sand—with little and bad water, in twenty-two hours, eighteen and a half of which was actual marching time. The horses were in such good condition at the end of the ride, that after one day's rest the men started back, and made the home trip at the rate of sixty miles a day. In 1880, Lieutenant Robertson, First Cavalry, rode from Fort Lapwai to Fort Walla Walla, one hundred and two miles, over the snow, deep in places, in twenty-three and a half hours; and starting next morning, rode back in two days. These are but a few out of scores of equal performances. The keen appreciation of pace and of the ability of the animals ridden in such feats is marked. Men who can do work like this and come in fresh, must be consummate horsemen.

"In constant association with the cavalryman comes that most faithful servant—the only good Indian except a dead one—the Indian scout." To these can now be added the remarkable trip of Gen. Guy Henry's (Buffalo), Ninth Cavalry, last winter, to the relief of Pine Ridge after "Wounded Knee," over ninety-six miles in the night, a fight at daylight after arrival, a light breakfast—rush to the successful aid of the Seventh at "the Mission" afterward, and a return at night after two days almost continually in the saddle; two severe fights, and not a *sore back horse in the outfit.*

Such is the regular army of U. S., the nucleus of the Grand Army of Emergency, which is commanded by such experienced men as Generals Schofield, Howard, Gibbon, Brook, Wheaton, Henry, Ruger, Sumner, Forsyth, Carr, Merritt and the strategist of the late Indian war, General Nelson A. Miles.

A POSITION DIFFICULT TO ATTAIN.—A "PLAINS CELEBRITY."—A TITLE IMPERISHABLE.

To gain great local and national fame as a "plains celebrity" in the days of old was not an easy task; rather one of the most competitive struggles that a young man could possibly engage in. The vast, comparatively unknown, even called Great American Desert of twenty-five and thirty years ago was peopled only by the descendants of the sturdy pioneers of the then Far West—Illinois, Missouri, Arkansas, Iowa, Minnesota, Kansas, etc., born, raised, and used to hardships and danger, and attracted only the resolute, determined adventurers of the rest of the world, seeking an outlet for pent-up natures, imbued with love of daring adventure. Hundreds of men achieved local, and great numbers national fame for the possession of every manly quality that goes to make up the romantic hero of that once dark and bloody ground. When it is brought to mind the work engaged in, the carving out of the advance paths for the more domestically inclined settler, of the dangers and excitements of hunting and trapping, of carrying dispatches, stage driving, freighting cargoes of immense value, guiding successfully the immense wagon trains, gold hunting, it is easy to conceive what a class of sturdy, adventurous young spirits entered the arena to struggle in a daily deadly dangerous game to win the "bubble reputation." When such an army of the best human material battled for supremacy, individual distinction gained by the unwritten law of unprejudiced *popular* promotion, possessed a value that made its acquirer a "plains celebrity," stamped indelibly with an *honored title* rarely possessed unless fairly, openly, and justly won—a prize so pure that its ownership, while envied, crowned the victor with the friendship, following and admiration of the contestants. Thus Boone, Crockett, Carson, Beal, Fremont, Cody, Bridger, Kinman, Hicock, Cosgrove, Comstock, Frank North, and others, will live in the romance, the poetry, and history of their each distinctive work forever. The same spirit and circumstances have furnished journalists innumerable, who in the West imbibed the sterling qualities they afterward used to such effect. Notably Henry M. Stanley, who (in 1866) saw the rising sun of the young empire that stretches to the Rockies; General Greeley, of Arctic fame (now of signal service), and the equally scientific explorer, Lieut. Schwatka, passed their early career in the same school, and often followed "the trail" led by "BUFFALO BILL"; Finerty (of the "Chicago Times"); "Modoc" Fox, and O'Kelly (of the "New York Herald"), 1876; while last year new blood among the scribblers was initiated to their baptism of fire by Harries (of "Washington Star"), McDonough ("New York World"), Bailey (of "Inter Ocean"), brave young Kelly (of the "Lincoln Journal"), Cressy (of the "Omaha Bee"), Seymour ("Chicago Herald"), and Allen (of the "New York Herald"), present in the battle, who were honored by three cheers from "Old White Top" Forsythe, gallant 7th Cavalry, the day after the battle of "Wounded Knee," as they went charging over Wolf Creek to what came near being a crimson day, to the fight "down at the Mission." That there are still "successors to every king" is assured by the manly scouts so prominent in last winter's rehearsal of past (hoped no more future) frontier dramas in such men as FRANK GRUARD, now the most celebrated of the present employed army scouts; of "LITTLE BAT," true as steel, and active as the cougar; PHILIP WELLS, LOUIS SHANGRAU, "BIG BAPTISTE," and JOHN SHANGRAU; while the friendly Indians furnish such grand material for any future necessity as "NO NECK," Major "SWORD," "RED SHIRT," and "YANKTON CHARLEY."

BILL CODY.—(BY AN OLD COMRADE.)

You bet I know him, pardner, he 'aint no circus fraud,
He's western born and western bred, if he has been late abroad;
I knew him in the days way back, beyond Missouri's flow,
When the country round was nothing but a huge Wild Western Show,
When the Injuns were as thick as fleas, and the man who ventured through
The sand hills of Nebraska had to fight the hostile Sioux;
These were hot times, I tell you; and we all remember still
The days when Cody was a scout, and all the men knew Bill.

I knew him first in Kansas, in the days of '68,
When the Cheyennes and Arapahoes were wiping from the slate
Old scores against the settlers, and when men who wore the blue,
With shoulder straps and way up rank, were glad to be helped through
By a bearer of dispatches, who knew each vale and hill
From Dakota down to Texas, and his other name was Bill.

I mind me too of '76, the time when Cody took
His scouts upon the Rosebud; along with General Crook;
When Custer's Seventh rode to their death for lack of some such aide
To tell them that the sneaking Sioux knew how to ambuscade;
I saw Bill's fight with "Yellow Hand," you bet it was a "mill,"
He downed him well at thirty yards, and all the men cheered Bill.

They tell me that the women folk now take his word as laws,
In them days laws were mighty skerce, and hardly passed with squaws,
But many a hardy settler's wife and daughter used to rest
More quietly because they knew of Cody's dauntless breast;
Because they felt from Laramie way down to Old Fort Sill,
Bill Cody was a trusted scout, and all their men knew Bill.

I haven't seen him much of late, how does he bear his years?
They say he's making ducats now from shows and not from "steers,"
He used to be a judge of "horns," when poured in a tin cup,
And left the wine to tenderfeet, and men who felt "way up."
Perhaps he cracks a bottle now, perhaps he's had his fill.
Who cares, Bill Cody was a scout, and all the world knows Bill.

To see him in his trimmins, he can't hardly look the same,
With laundered shirt and diamonds, as if "he run a game,"
He didn't wear biled linen then, or flash up diamond rings,
The royalties he dreamed of then were only pasteboard kings,
But those who sat behind the Queens were apt to get their fill,
In the days when Cody was a scout, and all the men knew Bill.

Gridiron Club,
Washington, D. C., Feb. 28th, 1891.

WM. E. ANNIN,
Lincoln (Neb.) Journal.

GHOST-DANCES IN THE WEST.

Origin and Development of the Messiah Craze and the Ghost-Dance.

Pine Ridge Reservation.—There have often happened, in the history of the human race, incidents that were regarded at the time as most trivial, but have later developed into such important and serious questions as to engage the minds of many learned men in their solution.

That there is some special reason for the series of frenzied dances and incantations which have been continued from time to time in remote portions of the Sioux reservations, no one will deny. It is scarcely probable that a people who own horses and cattle would suddenly, without the slightest warning, return almost to a man to the execution of a dance which is so weird and peculiar, so superstitious and spirit-like, as to rival the far-famed Sun Dance.

OGALLALLA CHIEFS.
PINE RIDGE—SIOUX CAMPAIGN, 1891.

This special reason is found in the simple truths of Christianity as taught by a missionary in Utah, but which were distorted to conform with Indian mythology. It was when the medicine men and politicians in the nation began to enlarge upon the wrongs suffered at the hands of the whites, the scarcity of food, the presence of the military, that its general aspect was changed from a sacred rite to a warlike demonstration.

The Indians located in the Dakotas have been in the habit of visiting the Utes and Arapahoes every summer for the purpose of trading and hunting en route. While the Sioux are unable to converse with these tribes, means of communication is possible through the medium of the sign-language, which is well understood by all Indians throughout the West. Keeps the Battle (Ki-cizapi Tawa) told me a few days ago that it was during the visit of the Pine Ridge Sioux last July that he first heard of the coming of the new Messiah. He related the following story:

"Scarcely had my people reached the Ute village when we heard of a white preacher whom the Utes held in the highest esteem, who told a beautiful dream or vision of the coming of a great and good red man. This strange person was to set aright the wrongs of my people; he could restore to us our game and hunting-grounds, was so powerful that every wish or word he gave utterance to became fulfilled.

"His teachings had a strange effect upon the Utes, and, in obedience to the commands of this man, they began a Messiah Dance. My people did not pay much attention to this dance at first, and it was not until we took our departure that the matter began to weigh heavily upon the minds of a number in the party. As we left the Ute camp the minister stood with uplifted hands and invoked the blessing of the Great Spirit upon us. He told us to look for the coming of the Saviour; and assured us that he would soon and unexpectedly arrive. He further cautioned us to be watching and ready to accompany him to the bright and Happy Hunting Grounds, to be sorry for our sins, to institute a Messiah Dance among our people at Pine Ridge, and to keep up this dance until the Lord himself shall appear."

When the Ghost or Messiah Dance was first given on Pine Ridge Reservation by the Sioux who had been in Utah on a visit to the Ute Indians, there were many on-lookers. These became interested as the dance proceeded, for such was its influence upon a beholder that he felt an irresistible desire to join the circle.

The largest camp of the dancers prior to the departure for the North was located upon Wounded Knee Creek. Other camps of considerable extent existed upon White Clay Creek, four miles from the agency headquarters, upon Porcupine and Medicine Root streams. Nearly five hundred persons were leaping up and down, or rolling upon the earth, at one time, in an enormous circle. The earth is packed as firm as a cemented cellar bottom, so rendered by the thousands of feet that stamped furiously upon the surface, and for a space of three hundred and fifty feet in diameter there is not a vestige of grass, nor the indication of the smallest shrub.

"SITTING BULL."
The celebrated Uncapapa Sioux Chief, killed in 1891.

When the medicine men took the Ghost Dance under their charge one man was appointed "High Priest," to have entire control of the ceremonies. His four assistants were likewise invested with power to start or stop the dance at will. They were given authority to punish any person who should refuse to obey their commands.

While the priests are employed in their prayers, the squaws make a good-sized sweat-house. Poles are stuck in the ground and the tops bent together and securely tied. These saplings are strong enough to bear the weight of several hundred pounds. Over the framework are heaped blankets and robes to such a thickness that no smoke or steam can pass from the interior. A fire is started in a hole in the ground several feet from the small entrance to the sweat-lodge, and twenty or thirty good-sized stones are placed therein to be heated. When these rocks have become sufficiently hot, the young men who are to partake of the bath, strip with the exception of the breech clout, and crawl through the door. They seat themselves in a circle, with their feet toward the center and their backs against the sides of the lodge. The attendant shoves some of the hot stones inside, and the young men pour water from a hide bucket upon the little stone heap. Steam and vapor arise, completely filling the inclosure. The attendant has meanwhile covered the opening so that no air from the outside may penetrate. As the vapor condenses, the attendant thrusts more stones within, and thus the operation is continued as long as the youths can stand the confinement. The pipe is also smoked during the sweat. When the young men issue from their bath the perspiration is fairly streaming from every pore. If it is not cold weather they plunge into a pool in the creek near by, but if it be chilly they wrap blankets about their bodies.

Several sweat-houses are erected in order to prepare the young men for the dance. When a good number of young men, say fifty or sixty, have thus prepared themselves, the high priest and his assistants come forward. The high priest wears eagle-feathers in his hair, and a short skirt reaches from his waist nearly to his knees. The assistants are dressed in a similar manner, but wear no ornaments other than the eagle feathers. The dancers wear no ornaments whatever and enter the circle without their blankets, many of them only wearing their ordinary clothes.

That Indians should lay aside all ornaments and finery and dance without the trappings which they so dearly love, proves conclusively that some powerful religious influence is at work.

In their other dances, the Omaha, the Old Woman, the Sun, and War Dances, feathers and bangles, weapons, herbs or painted and plaited grasses, porcupine quills, horses' tails and bits of furskins, necklaces, bells, silver disks, etc., are worn in great profusion.

JOHN SHANGRAU.
Government Scout, Guide and Interpreter in charge of the Military Hostages.

The candidates for "conversion" do not fast, as has been stated by several writers who have not thoroughly investigated the subject. After they have come forth from the sweat-house they are ready to enter the sacred circle. The high priest runs quickly from the village to the open space of ground, five or six hundred yards distant, and stationing himself near the sacred tree, begins his chant as follows:

"Hear, hear you all persons!

"Come, hurry up and dance, and when you have finished running in the circle, tell these people what you have seen in the spirit land.

"I myself have been in the spirit land, and have seen many strange and beautiful things, all of which the great Wakantanka rules over, and which my eyes tell me are good and true."

As the speaker proceeds the men and women leave their tepees and crowd to the dance-ground. They form two or three circles, according to the number of persons who wish to participate, and, grasping hands with fingers interlocked ("Indian grip"), the circles begin to move around toward the left. They rub their palms in dust or sand to prevent slipping, for it is considered unlucky for one to break connections.

The sacred tree needs a few words of explanation. It is a nearly straight sapling thirty or forty feet high, trimmed of branches to a height of several feet. To the topmost twigs is attached a small white flag or canvas strip, supposed to be an emblem of purity, together with some of colors. The base of the tree is wrapped with rushes and flags to a thickness of about five feet. Between the reeds the dancers from time to time thrust little gifts or peace-offerings. These offerings are supposed to allay the anger of the Great Spirit, and are given in perfectly good faith by the poor natives. They consist of small pieces of calico, bags of tobacco, or pipes. During the heat of excitement, those worshipers most deeply affected cut small particles of flesh from their arms, and thrust these, also, between the rushes of the holy tree.

Henry Hunter (The Weasel "Itonkasan") informs me that after the dance had been running some days, the rushes covering the base of the tree were literally besmeared with human blood!

As the circle moves toward the left, the priest and his assistants cry out loudly for the dancers to stop a moment. As they pause he raises his hand toward the west, and, upon all the people acting similarly, begins the following remarkable prayer:

"Great Spirit, look at us now. Grandfather and Grandmother have come. All these good people are going to see Wakantanka, but they will be brought safely back to earth. Everything that is good you will see there, and you can have these things by going there. All things that you hear there will be holy and true, and when you return you can tell your friends how spiritual it is."

As he prays, the dancers cry aloud with all the fervor of religious fanatics. They moan and sob, many of them exclaiming: "Great Father, I want you to have pity upon me."

One can scarcely imagine the terrible earnestness of these people. George E. Bartlett, the United States Deputy Marshal of this district, and Mr. Sweeney, one of the Agency schoolteachers, the chief herder, Mr. John Darr, and others, have informed me

"JOHNNY BURKE NO NECK."
Found on the Battle Field of Wounded Knee after the annihilation of Big Foot's Band.

that during their extended experience on the Agency, of many years' duration, they have witnessed many of these dances. They describe the scene of the dance, especially at night, as most weird and ghostlike. The fires are very large, and shed a bright reflection all around. The breasts of the worshipers heave with emotion; they groan and cry as if they were suffering great agony, and as the priest begs them to ask great Wakantanka to forgive their sins, such a cry of despair and anguish arises as to deeply affect even the whites present. Bartlett said that, in his opinion, men could not be more in dead earnest nor pray harder than did these poor children of the plains.

After prayer and weeping, and offerings have been made to the sacred pole, the dance is started again. The dancers go rather slowly at first, and as the priests in the center begin to shout and leap about, the dancers partake of the enthusiasm. Instead of moving with a regular step, each person jumps backward and forward, up and down, as hard as he or she can without relinquishing their hold upon their neighbor's hand. One by one the dancers fall out of the ranks, some staggering like drunken men, others wildly rushing here and there, almost bereft of reason. Many fall upon the earth to writhe about as if possessed of demons, while blinded women throw their clothes over their heads and run through brush or against trees. The priests are kept busy waving eagle-feathers in the faces of the most violent worshipers. The feather is considered sacred, and its use, together with the mesmeric glance and motion of the priest, soon causes the victim to fall into a trance or deep sleep. Whether this sleep is real or feigned the writer does not pretend to say, but sufficiently deep is it that whites visiting the dance have been unable to rouse the sleepers by jest or blow.

Unquestionably the priests exercise an influence over the more susceptible of the dancers akin to hypnotism. One of the young men, who danced in the ghost circle twenty times, told me that the priest:

"Looked very hard at us. Some of the young men and women could not withstand his snake-like gaze, and did whatever he told them."

If this does not describe the manner in which a "professor" of mesmerism influences his pupils, nothing can.

Regarding what is seen by the converts when in the spirit land there is much speculation. I have secured interviews with three prominent chiefs touching upon this matter, and before relating what they told me I wish to call especial attention to the strong resemblance of their visions to the teachings of the Saviour in the New Testament.

CHIEF "NO NECK."

Ogallalla Sioux. Famous Warrior. A Friendly. A Leading Government Scout in Last Campaign.

"When I fell in the trance a great and grand eagle came and carried me over a great hill, where there was a village such as we used to have before the whites came into the country. The tepees were all of buffalo hides, and we made use of the bow and arrow, there being nothing of white man's manufacture in the beautiful land. Nor were any whites permitted to live there. The broad and fertile lands stretched in every direction, and were most pleasing to my eyes.

"I was taken into the presence of the great Messiah, and he spoke to me these words:

"My child, I am glad to see you. Do you want to see your children and relations who are dead?'

"I replied: 'Yes, I would like to see my relations who have been dead a long time.' The God then called my friends to come up to where I was. They appeared riding the finest horses I ever saw, dressed in superb and most brilliant garments, and seeming very happy. As they approached, I recognized the playmates of my childhood, and I ran forward to embrace them while the tears of joy ran down my cheeks.

"LITTLE EMMA."

Indian Girl. Daughter of the Ogallalla Chief, "Lone Wolf."

"We all went together to another village, where there were very large lodges of buffalo hide, and there held a long talk with the great Wakantanka. Then he had some squaws prepare us a meal of many herbs, meat, and wild fruits and 'wasna' (pounded beef and choke-berries). After we had eaten, the Great Spirit prayed for our people upon the earth, and then we all took a smoke out of a fine pipe ornamented with the most beautiful feathers and porcupine quills. Then we left the city and looked into a great valley where there were thousands of buffalo, deer, and elk feeding.

"After seeing the valley, we returned to the city, the Great Spirit speaking meanwhile. He told me that the earth was now *bad* and *worn out;* that we needed a new dwelling-place where the rascally whites could not disturb us. He further instructed me to return to my people, the Sioux, and say to them that if they would be constant in the dance, and pay no attention to the whites, he would shortly come to their aid. If the high-priests would make for the dancers medicine-shirts and pray over them, no harm could come to the wearer; that the bullets of any whites that desired to stop the Messiah Dance would fall to the ground without doing any one harm, and the person firing such shots would drop dead. He said that he had prepared a hole in the ground filled with hot water and fire for the reception of all white men and non-believers. With these parting words I was commanded to return to earth."

The above story was related by Lone Wolf, as heard by him from a ghost dancer. It is a literal translation.

Music of the Dance.—There are intermissions every hour in the progress of the dance, and during these pauses several pipes are passed around. Each smoker blows a cloud upward toward the supposed dwelling-place of the Messiah. He inhales deep draughts of the fragrant smoke of red willow-bark into his lungs, blows it out through his nose, and then passes the pipe to his neighbor.

The songs are sung without accompaniment of a drum, as is customary in the other dances. All sing in unison, and the notes, although wild and peculiar, being in a minor key, do not lack melody. The Weasel (Itonkasan) has given me the following two songs as sung by his people during the dance.

The words sung in Sioux are:

Ina he kuye misunkala ceya omaniye-e. Ina he kuye. Ate he lo. Ate he lo.

As translated by Deputy U. S. Marshal Bartlett, this is:

Come here my mother; my younger brother is walking and crying. Come here my mother; here is the father, here is the father.

Here are the notes of another song:

To this strain are used the words:

Ate he ye lo, canupawan ci ci ca hu pi ca yani pi kta lo. Ate he ye lo. Ate he ye lo.

Which in English are:

This the father said, he brings the pipe* for you, and you will live. This the father said, this the father said.

"KICKING BEAR."
Ogallalla Sioux, War Chief of the Messiah Craze, Fighting Chief of Ghost Dancers.

Just after the dancers have been crying and moaning about their sins the priests strike up the first song, in which all join, singing with deafening loudness. Some man or woman may be at this moment at the tree, with his or her arms thrown about the rushes, sobbing as if the heart would break; or another may be walking and crying, wringing his hands, or going through some motion to indicate the deepest sorrow for his transgressions. So the singer cries aloud to his mother to be present and aid him. The appeal to the father refers, of course, to the Messiah, and its use in this connection is supposed to give emphasis to the demand for the mother's presence, and hasten her coming.

The second song requires a longer explanation. It expresses in brief the goodness of the father. Some one of the dancers has come to life from the trance, and has just related his or her experience in the other world. The high-priest, enlarging upon the importance of this fact, runs about the interior of the circle handing several pipes around, exclaiming that these pipes were received direct from the Great Spirit, and that all who smoke them will live. The people are worked up to such a pitch of religious frenzy that their minds are now willing to receive any utterance as truth indisputable, so they pass around the pipes, singing the song meanwhile. The repetition of the words, "This the father said," gives more weight to the song.

The vision of Little Horse is still more remarkable. Through the Weasel he said:

"Two holy eagles transported me to the Happy Hunting Grounds. They showed me the Great Messiah there, and as I looked upon his fair countenance I wept, for there were nail-prints in his hands and feet where the cruel whites had once fastened him to a large cross There was a small wound in his side also, but as he kept himself covered with a beautiful mantle of feathers this wound only could be seen when he shifted his blanket. He insisted that we continue the dance and promised me that no whites should enter his city nor partake of the good things

*The use of the pipe is ceremonial and holy.

"PLENTY HORSES,"
Who, with "Scatt r," and "Revenge," were leading B aves with "Short Bull" and "Kicking Bea ."

he had prepared for the Indians. The earth, he said, was now worn out and it should be re-peopled.

"He had a long beard and long hair, and was the most handsome man I ever looked upon."

Philanthropists, while meaning well, from a lack of knowledge of the nature of an Indian, treat him in such a sympathetic manner—often selecting the most worthless and lazy Indians to bestow their favors upon—that he becomes puffed up with his own importance. Egotism leads to insolence, and insolence gets him into serious trouble with the agency employes and Westerners in general. The churches are all doing a good work, and it is not my purpose to say much against them, but they should work in unison, not against each other. The Indian cannot understand how so many beliefs could spring from one good book, and, naturally suspicious, when he hears one missionary speak disparagingly of the salvation afforded by a rival church, concludes the whole set are humbugs.

When the commission visited the agency in the summer of 1889, for the purpose of securing signatures to the treaty whereby the Sioux relinquished claim to several million acres of their land, a number of promises were made by the commissioners which were never kept. Not so with the Indians themselves. As they sat about their tepee fires and discussed the affairs of their nation, they often wondered why the increase in rations did not come, why the presents were so long delayed.

An Indian never forgets a promise.

Can it be wondered, then, that the Sioux lost what little remaining faith they had in the whites?

As they brooded over their wrongs, the scarcity of rations, and miserable treatment, imagine with what joy they hailed the coming of Him who was to save and rescue them. How they hoped and prayed, only to be deluded and again cast into the depths of despair! Even this last boon and comfort was refused by their conquerors; for no sooner had the news of the coming Saviour reached Washington when orders were issued to suppress the worship of any Indian who should dare to pray to his God after the dictates of his own conscience, or at least to stop the Ghost Dances.

"SHORT BULL."
Bru e Si ux—Leader of th Ghost Dancers, 'High [illegible]

[*The above is condensed from* ILLUSTRATED AMERICA, *and is in many respects very accurate, but the compiler gives it without comment, as the whole matter has yet to be investigated to get at bottom facts.*—J. M. B.

THE ORIGIN OF THE NORTH-AMERICAN INDIAN.

A Legend.—Respectfully Dedicated to Lieut. F. H. HARDIE, 3d Cavalry U. S. A.

There is a legend 'mong the plumed race,
Which strange though be, their origin does trace
To days primeval, when the mighty plan,
With touch most wonderful was crowned with man.

With air oracular it has been told
By Chieftains, nature-wise, so very old,
Who, solemn sworn, as were their fathers too,
This wonderful tradition seal as true.

It was the season when the sighing breeze
Bestrewed the ground with Autumn-painted leaves—
When Nature robed herself in rich array,
Her vesture interwove with sad and gay.

The buffalo, the elk and fallow deer
In quiet grazed, with naught to harm or fear,
For yet unborn the stealthy hunter foe,
Unwrought the murd'rous flint and arched bow.

Sublimity and grandeur did pervade
The sun-tipped mountain-top and forest shade,
As silence, most profound, with thoughtful train,
The Universe spell-bound with magic chain.

Lo, the Great Spirit gazed the scene upon
And saw perfection in all things but one;
There were the hills and dales, and seas and land,
And landscapes everywhere supremely grand,
And fish and fowl, and beast on mount and plain,
But who t' enjoy and over all to reign?

So from the border of a brooklet's way,
Lo, the Great Spirit took a piece of clay,
And with a touch and look both sad and sweet,
Did mould it into form most exquisite.

Then breathed He on this thing symmetrical formed,
When lo, it into life and being warmed,
And in the presence of its Maker stood,
A female beauty—type of womanhood.

* * * * *

Night came: the constellations bright,
Shed o'er the earth their distant, twinkling light
And through their mellow coruscated sheen
Cast pearly tears upon this beauty-queen,
Who, tired, reposed in quiet on the ground,
With senses wrapped in balmy sleep profound.

How passing lovely, how enchanting she,
Pure, spotless as her own virginity,
Like "lily of the vale" or budding rose
Upon the parent—Earth, in sweet repose.

In semblance of a star was one above,
Who, gazing on this beauty, fell in love,
For who, or which, or what such charms could see
And not be filled with love's own ecstacy?

And, as the story goes, this brilliant star
Which did outshine the other ones by far,
Assuming manly form, rushed from above,
And clasped the maiden in th' embrace of love.

This flaming star, or sprite, or man, or what,
With fullest unrestraint and passions hot,
Imprinted fiery kiss, again, again,
Before she could her liberty regain.

The maid so courted by the man-like flame,
Blushed deep, through native modesty, not shame
These blushes overspread the virgin, lo,
Were brazen by the wooer's ardent glow,
And thus became enstamped indelibly,
A signet royal of her modesty.

From her—To-ká-pá*—that her cherished name.
The red man of the Western Prairies came.

G. C. C.

* To-ká-pá (pronounced as if spelled To-káł -páh) is a word in the Teton dialogue of the Dakota or Sioux language, signifying *first-born.*

LATE MILITARY REFERENCES.

During the last year much has been said relative to CODY, the Wild West, Indians, etc., of an uncalled-for nature, and as "an open confession is good for the soul," we freely admit being annoyed. Who likes their *motives* misconstrued? Who can possibly believe it incompatible with honor to go the even tenor of your inclinations, when none but the hypercritical can possibly find a flaw? If it is correct that "he who preaches the gospel must live by the gospel," most certainly must he who has never held an interest in a Golconda live by that line of enterprise he finds most compatible to embark in if it be within the bounds of law, order and morality. Therefore it is that this compilation is rendered necessarily pointedly personal in eulogistic extracts as a cross-counter, when a more modest presentation of the Wild West's status would be justly considered as meeting the requirements. But many noted instances occur to the writer where the purpose would have been best served by the plain statement of facts. The aim of existence is to achieve happiness, and nine-tenths of mankind would be happy if the other tenth would attend to their own business, or seek information before exploding. To explain a mooted question! GENERAL CODY holds his commission in the NATIONAL GUARD of the United States (State of Nebraska), an honorable position, and as high as he can possibly attain. *His connection with the Regular United States Army* has covered a continuous period of *fifteen years*, and desultory connection of thirty years, in the most troublous era of that superb corp's Western history, as Guide, Scout, and Chief of Scouts—a position unknown in any other service, and for the confidential nature of which see General Dodge's extract on page 8. This privileged position, and the nature of its services in the past, may be more fully appreciated when it is understood that it commanded, beside horses, subsistence, and quarters, $10 per day ($3,650 per year), all expenses, and for special service, or "life and death" volunteer missions, special rewards of from $100 to $500 for carrying a single dispatch, and brought its holder the confidence of Commanding Generals, the fraternal friendship of the Commissioned Officers, the idolization of the ranks, and the universal respect and consideration of the hardy pioneers and settlers of the West. "BILL" CODY'S children can point with pride to recorded services under the following officers of world-wide and national fame :

General Sherman	General Smith	General Royall
" Miles	" King	" Penrose
" Crook	" Van Vliet	" Brisbin
" Carr	" Anson Mills	" Sandy Forsyth
" Augur	" Reynolds	" Palmer
" Bankhead	" Harney	" Dudley
" Fry	" Greeley	" Gibbon
" Crittenden	" Sheridan	" Canby
" Merritt	" Terry	" Blunt
" Switzer	" Emory	" Hayes
" Tony Forsyth	" Custer	" Guy Henry
" Duncan	" Ord	" Hazen
" Rucker	" Hancock	And others.

The extracts on the following pages speak for themselves, and will form interesting reading as authenticated references:

FROM GEN. "PHIL" SHERIDAN'S AUTOBIOGRAPHY.

GENERAL SHERIDAN refers to his meeting "BUFFALO BILL." "He undertakes a dangerous task," chapter xii, p. 281—289, in his autobiography, published in 1888. The world-renowned cavalry commander maintained continuous friendly relations with this old scout, even to social correspondence, friendly assistance, and recognition in his present enterprise up to the year of his death. After relating his conception of the *first winter campaign* against Indians on the then uninhabited and bleak plains, in the winter of 1868, he says, "The difficulties and hardships to be encountered had led several experienced officers of the army and some frontiersmen like old Jim Bridger, the famous scout and guide of earlier days, to discourage the project. Bridger even went so far as to come out from St. Louis to discourage the attempt. I decided to go in person, bent on showing the Indians that they were not secure from punishment because of inclement weather—an ally on which they had hitherto relied with much assurance. We started, and the very first night a blizzard struck us and carried away our tents. The gale was so violent that they could not be put up again; the rain and snow drenched us to the skin. Shivering from *wet and cold I took refuge under a wagon*, and there spent such a miserable night that, when morning came, the gloomy predictions of old man Bridger and others rose up before me with greatly increased force. The difficulties were now fully realized, the blinding snow, mixed with sleet, the piercing wind, thermometer below zero—with green bushes only for fuel—occasioning intense suffering. Our numbers and companionship alone prevented us from being lost or perishing, a fate that stared in the face the frontiersmen, guides and scouts on their solitary missions.

"An important matter had been to secure competent guides for the different columns of troops, for, as I have said, the section of *country to be operated in was comparatively unknown*.

"In those days the railroad town of Hays City was filled with so-called 'Indian Scouts,' whose common boast was of having slain scores of redskins, but the real scout—that is, a guide and trailer knowing the habits of the Indians—was very scarce, and it was hard to find anybody familiar with the country south of the Arkansas, where the campaign was to be made. Still, about the various military posts there was some good material to select from, and we managed to employ several men, who, from their experience on the plains in various capacities, or from natural instinct and aptitude, soon became excellent guides and and courageous and valuable scouts, some of them, indeed, gaining much distinction. Mr. William F. Cody ('Buffalo Bill'), whose renown has since become world-wide, was one of the men thus selected. He received his sobriquet from his marked success in killing buffaloes to supply fresh meat to the construction parties on the Kansas-Pacific Railway. He had lived from boyhood on the plains and passed every experience ; herder, hunter, pony express rider, stage driver, wagon master in the quartermaster's department, and scout of the army, and was first brought to my notice by distinguishing himself in bringing me an important dispatch from Fort Larned to Fort Hays, a distance of sixty-five miles, through a section infested with Indians. The dispatch informed me that the Indians near Larned were preparing to decamp, and this intelligence required that certain orders should be carried to Fort Dodge, ninety-five miles south of Hays. This too being a particularly dangerous route—several couriers having been killed on it—it was impossible to get one of the various "Petes," "Jacks," or "Jims" hanging around Hays City to take my communication. Cody, learning of the strait I was in, manfully came to the rescue, and proposed to make the trip to Dodge, though he had just finished his long and perilous ride from Larned. I gratefully accepted his offer, and after short rest, he mounted a fresh horse and hastened on his journey, halting but once to rest on the way, and then only for an hour, the stop being made at Coon Creek; where he got another mount from a troop of cavalry. At Dodge he took some sleep, and then continued on his own post—Fort Larned—with more dispatches. After resting at Larned, he was again in the saddle with tidings for me at Fort Hays, General Hazen sending him, this time, with word that the villages had fled to the south of the Arkansas. Thus, in all, Cody rode about 350 miles in less than sixty hours, and such an exhibition of endurance and courage at that time of the year, and in such weather, was more than enough to convince me that his services would be extremely valuable in the campaign, so I retained him at Fort Hays till the battalion of the Fifth Cavalry arrived, and then made him CHIEF OF SCOUTS."

Read through the fascinating book, "Campaigning with Crook (Major General George Crook, U. S. A.). and Stories of Army Life," due to the graphic and soldierly pen of Captain Charles King, of the U. S. Army; published only last year (1890).

Incidentally the author refers in various pages to COL. CODY as Scout, etc ., and testifies to the general esteem and affection in which "BUFFALO BILL" is held by the army.

The subjoined extracts from the book will give our readers an excellent idea of the military scout's calling and its dangers :

"By Jove! General," says "BUFFALO BILL," sliding backward down the hill, "now's our chance. Let our party mount here out of sight, and we'll cut those fellows off. Come down every other man of you."

Glancing behind me, I see CODY, TAIT and "CHIPS," with five cavalrymen, eagerly bending forward in their saddles, grasping carbine and rifle, every eye bent upon me, watching for the signal. Not a man but myself knows how near they are. That's right, close in, you beggars! Ten seconds more and you are on them! A hundred and twenty-five yards—a hundred—ninety— "Now, lads; in with you."

There's a rush, a wild ringing cheer; then bang, bang, bang! and in a cloud of dust, CODY and his men tumble in among them, "BUFFALO BILL" closing on a superbly accoutred warrior. It is the work of a minute; the Indian has fired and missed. CODY'S bullet tears through the rider's leg into the pony's heart, and they tumble in a confused heap on the prairie. The Cheyenne struggles to his feet for another shot, but CODY'S second bullet hits the mark. It is now close quarters, knife to knife. After a hand to hand struggle, CODY wins, and the young chief "YELLOW HAND," drops lifeless in his tracks after a hot fight. Baffled and astounded, for once in a lifetime beaten at their own game, their project of joining "SITTING BULL" nipped in the bud, they take hurried flight. But our chief is satisfied—"BUFFALO BILL" is radiant; his are the honors of the day. . . . . . . —*From Page* 35.

"BUFFALO BILL" AND "BUFFALO CHIPS."—*From Page* 111.

In all these years of campaigning, the Fifth Cavalry has had varied and interesting experience with a class of men of whom much has been written, and whose names, to readers of the dime novel and the *New York Weekly* style of literature, were familiar as household words; I mean the "Scouts of the Prairie," as they have been christened. Many thousands of our citizens have been to see "BUFFALO BILL'S" thrilling representations of the scenes of his life of adventure. To such he needs no introduction. and throughout our cavalry he is better known than any general except Miles or Crook.

A motley set they are as a class—these scouts; hard riding, hard swearing, hard drinking ordinarily, and not all were of unimpeachable veracity. But there was never a word of doubt or question in the Fifth when "BUFFALO BILL" came up for discussion. He was chief of scouts in Kansas and Nebraska in the campaign of 1868-69, when the hostiles were so completely used up by General Carr. He remained with us as chief scout until the regiment was ordered to Arizona to take its turn at the Apaches in 1871. Five years the regiment was kept among the rocks and deserts of that marvelous land of cactus and centipede; but when we came homeward across the continent and were ordered up to Cheyenne to take a hand in the Sioux war of 1876, the "SITTING BULL" campaign, the first addition to our ranks was "BUFFALO BILL" himself, who sprang from the Union Pacific train at Cheyenne, and was speedily exchanging greetings with an eager group of his old comrades, reinstated as chief scouts.

Of his services during the campaign that followed, a *dozen articles* might be written. One of the most thrilling incidents of our fight on the 17th of July with the Cheyenne Indians, on the War Bonnet, was when he killed the warrior "YELLOW HAND," in as plucky a single combat on both sides as is ever witnessed. The Fifth had a genuine affection for Bill; he was a tried and true comrade—one who for cool daring and judgment had no superior. He was a beautiful horseman, an unrivaled shot, and as a scout unequaled. We had tried them all—Hualpais and Tontos in Arizona; half-breeds on the great plains. We had followed Custer's old guide, "California Joe," in Dakota, met handsome Bill Hickox ("Wild Bill") in the Black Hills; trailed for weeks after Crook's favorite, Frank Gruard, with "Little Bat" and "Big Baptiste," three good ones, all over the Big Horn and Powder River country; hunted Nez Perces with Cosgrove and his Shoshones among the Yellowstone mountains, and listened to Crawford's yarns and rhymes in many a bivouac in the Northwest. They were all noted men in their way, but Bill Cody was the paragon.

This time it is not my purpose to write of him, but for him, of another whom I have not yet named.

James White was his name; a man little known east of the Missouri, but on the plains he was "Buffalo Bill's" shadow. I had met him for the first time at the McPherson station in the Platte Valley, 1871, when he came to me with a horse, and the simple introduction that he was a friend of Cody's. Long afterward we found how true and staunch a friend, for when Cody joined us at Cheyenne as chief scout, he brought White with him as assistant, and Bill's recommendation secured his immediate employment.

On many a long day's march after that White rode by my side along the flanks of the column, and I got to know him well. A simpler-minded, a gentler frontiersman never lived. He was modesty and courtesy itself, conspicuous mainly because of two or three unusual traits for his class—he never drank, I never heard him swear, and no man ever heard him lie.

For years he had been Cody's faithful follower, half servant, half "pardner." He was Bill's "Fidus Achates;" Bill was his adoration. They had been boys together, and the hero worship of extreme youth was simply intensified in the man. He copied Bill's dress, his gait, his carriage, his speech—everything he could copy; he let his long yellow hair fall low upon his shoulders in wistful imitation of Bill's glossy brown curls. He took more care of Bill's guns and horses than he did of his own, and so, when he finally claimed, one night at Laramie, the right to be known by some other title than simple Jim White—something descriptive, as it were, of his attachment for Cody, and lifelong devotion to his idol, "Buffalo Bill," a grim quartermaster (Morton of the Ninth Infantry) dubbed him "Buffalo Chips," and the name was a fixture. His story was a brief one after that episode. We launched out from Laramie on the 22d of June, and through all the vicissitudes of the campaign that followed, he was always near the Fifth. On the Yellowstone Cody was compelled to bid us a reluctant farewell to join General Terry.

A great loss to us was "BUFFALO BILL." He left his "pardner," Jim White, with us to finish the campaign as scout; and we little thought that those two sworn friends were meeting for the last time on earth when "BUFFALO CHIPS" bade good-bye to "BUFFALO BILL." "CHIPS" remained in his capacity as scout, though he seemed sorely to miss his "pardner."

It was just two weeks after that we struck the Sioux at Slim Buttes, something of which I told you in a former chapter. You may remember that the Fifth had ridden in haste to the relief of Major Mills, who had surprised the Indians away in our front early Saturday morning, had whipped them in panicky confusion out of their "tepees" into the neighboring rocks, and then had to fight on the defensive against ugly odds until we rode in to the rescue. As the head of our column jogged in among the lodges, and General Carr directed us to keep on down to face the bluffs to the south, Mills pointed to a ravine opening out into the village, with the warning. "Look out for that gully; there are Indians hidden there, and they've knocked over some of my men."

Everybody was too busy just then to pay much attention to two or three wounded Indians in a hole. We were sure of getting them when wanted. So, placing a couple of sentries where they could warn stragglers away from its front, we formed line along the south and west of the captured village, and got everything ready to resist the attack we knew they would soon make in full force.

General Crook had arrived on the scene, and, while we were waiting for "Lo" to resume the offensive, some few scouts and packers started in to have a little fun "rousting out them Injuns." Half a dozen soldiers got permission to go over and join in while the rest of us were hungrily hunting about for something to eat. The next thing, we heard a volley from the ravine, and saw the scouts and packers scattering for cover. One soldier held his ground—shot dead. Another moment, and it became apparent that not one or two, but a dozen Indians were crouching somewhere in that narrow gorge, and the move to get them out assumed proportions. Lieutenant Clark, of General Crook's staff, sprang into the entrance, carbine in hand, and a score of cavalrymen followed, while the scouts and others went cautiously along either bank, peering warily into the cave-like darkness at the head. A squad came tearing over, just as a second volley came from the concealed foe, and three more of our men dropped, bleeding, in their tracks. Now our people were fairly aroused, and officers and men by dozens hurried to the scene. The misty air rang with shots, and the chances looked bad for those redskins. Just at this moment, as I was running over from the western side, I caught sight of "CHIPS" on the opposite crest. All alone, he was cautiously making his way, on hands and knees, toward the head of the ravine, where he could look down upon the Indians beneath. As yet he was protected from their fire by the bank itself—his lean form distinctly outlined against the eastern sky. He reached a stunted tree that grew on the very edge of the gorge, and there he halted, brought his rifle close under his shoulder, in readiness to aim, and then raised himself slowly to his feet, lifting his head higher, higher, as he peered over. Suddenly a quick, eager light shone in his face, a sharp movement of his rifle, as though he were about to raise it to his shoulder, when, bang!—a puff of white smoke floated up from the head of the ravine, "CHIPS" sprang up convulsively in the air, clasping his hands to his breast, and with one startled, agonizing cry, "Oh, my God, boys!" plunged heavily forward on his face, down the slope—shot through the heart.

Two minutes more, what Indians were left alive were prisoners, and that costly experiment at an end. That evening, after the repulse of the grand attack of "ROMAN NOSE" and "STABBER'S" warriors, and, 'twas said, hundreds of "CRAZY HORSE'S" band, we buried poor "CHIPS," with our other dead, in a deep ravine. "WILD BILL," "CALIFORNIA JOE," COSGROVE, and "TEXAS JACK" have long since gone to their last account, but, among those who knew them, no scout was more universally mourned than "BUFFALO BILL'S" devoted friend, JIM WHITE.

THE SIOUX AND WILD WEST SHOWS.

Editorial from the New York Sun.

The permission granted by the Interior Department to BUFFALO BILL to engage 100 Sioux Indians for his Wild West Show, is a great victory for BILL. It is a more conspicuous success even than that which he achieved during the recent Pine Ridge Campaign, when, as Brigadier General commanding the Nebraska State forces, he received a written acknowledgment of his services from GEN. MILES. It has been accomplished, moreover, directly in the face of enormous obstacles which BUFFALO BILL found in his path; and the skill and success with which he surmounted them are proportionately great. First he took some of his performing braves to Washington to show the refining and ennobling influences which European travel had had upon them. Then, when the Sioux troubles broke out, and threatened to wreck his plans, especially as it was charged that the complaints of some of his troupe had aggravated the tribal discontent, he found in that very disaster his opportunity, and hastening to the scene, he took care that none of his recent performers should be conspicuously hostile to the Government. His next step was to procure recommendations from army officers, showing SECRETARY NOBLE the military wisdom of allowing some of the young, restless Sioux braves to be taken away from the reservation, under his charge. The issue was then between BUFFALO BILL and the COMMISSIONER, and the former won.

To the crowned heads of Europe and other eminent patrons of the Wild West Show this great victory will be very welcome. And now, the best thing for COMMISSIONER MORGAN and the REV. DR. DORCHESTER to do is to accept the first chance to see the show. They will probably enjoy the spectacle, and be proud of the professional progress of their wards.

CHICAGO, DEC. 13.—R. P. Haslam, better known on the frontier as "Pony Bob," being one of the hard riders who carried the overland mail before a railway was pushed through to the Pacific coast, is in the city. He accompanied COLONEL CODY on his recent trip from Standing Rock agency for the capture of Sitting Bull. Bob is in receipt of a letter from COLONEL CODY expressing astonishment at the story that in his chase after Sitting Bill he wore a dress suit. Lieutenant G. W. Chadwick, who has been quoted as making such statements has also *telegraphed a denial*, stating that the other interviews with himself were garbled and misconstrued. He says in his telegram that COLONEL CODY did his duty conscientiously, bravely, and well, according to the accounts which he has received of the trip. He says he was not detailed to accompany COLONEL CODY, as stated in the interview, and that he never saw him till several days after CODY's return from the trip.—*Chicago Herald.*

AS "BUFFALO BILL" SEES IT.—HE THINKS IT LOOKS LIKE PEACE IN THE INDIAN COUNTRY.

"Buffalo Bill" telegraphs to the "New York Herald" from Pine Ridge Agency:

"IN THE FIELD, *Via Courier to Telegraph*, PINE RIDGE AGENCY, DAKOTA.

"NEW YORK HERALD:

"Your request for my opinion of the Indian situation is by reason of the complications and the changeable nature of the red man's mind and action a puzzler. Every hour brings out a new opinion. Indian history furnishes no similar situation.

"You must imagine about 5,000 Indians, an unusual proportion warriors, better armed than ever known before, hemmed in a cordon about sixteen miles in diameter, composed of over 3,000 troops, acting like a slowly closing drag net. This mass of Indians is now influenced by a percentage as despairingly desperate and fanatical as the late Big Foot party, under Short Bull and Kicking Bear. It contains also restrained neutrals, frightened and disaffected Ogallallas, hampered by the powerful Brules, backed by renegades and desperadoes from all other agencies. There are about twenty-five hundred acting and believed to be friendly Indians in and around the Agency.

"Such is the situation General Miles and the military confront. Any one of this undisciplined mass is able to precipitate a terrible conflict from the most unexpected quarter. Each of the component quantities is to be watched, to be measured, to be just to. In fact, it is a war with a most wily and savage people, yet the whites are restrained by a humane and peaceful desire to prevent bloodshed, and save a people from themselves. It is like cooling and calming a volcano. Ordinary warfare shows no parallel. General Miles seems to hold a firm grip on the situation. The Indians know him, express confidence in his honor, truth, and justice to them, and they fear his power and valor as well.

"As the matter now stands, he and they should be allowed, untrammeled even by a suggestion, to settle the affair, as no one not on the spot can appreciate the fearfully delicate position. The chaff must be sifted from the wheat, and in this instance the chaff must be threshed.

"At the moment, so far as words go, I would say it will be peace, but the smoldering spark is visible that may precipitate a terrible conflict any time in the next few days. However it ends, more and prompt attention should be paid in the future to the Sioux Indian; his rights, his complaints, and even his necessities. Respect and consideration should also be shown for the gallant little army, for it is the Indian and soldier who pay the most costly price in the end. I think it looks like peace, and if so, the greater the victory.

"W. F. CODY, 'BUFFALO BILL'."

THE SITUATION IN THE INDIAN COUNTRY A MARVEL OF MILITARY STRATEGY.

COL. W. F. CODY ("BUFFALO BILL") who is at Pine Ridge, telegraphs the following for the "New York Sun," which expresses his views of the present critical situation:

"The situation to-day, so far as military strategy goes, is one of the best marked triumphs known in the history of Indian campaigns. It speaks for itself, for the usual incidents to an Indian warfare, such as raids on settlers and wide spread devastation, have been wholly prevented. Only one white man has been killed outside the military circle. The presiding genius and his able aids have acted with all the cautious prowess of the hunter in surrounding and placing in a trap his dangerous game, at the same time recognizing the value of keeping the game imprisoned for future reasons. I speak, of course, of the campaign as originally intended to overawe and pacify the disaffected portion of the Ogallallas, Wassaohas, and Brules, the Big Foot affair at Wounded Knee Creek being an unlooked-for accident.

CREDITABLE TO GEN. MILES' REPUTATION.

"The situation to-day, with a desperate band corraled and the possibility of any individual fanatic running amuck is most critical, but the wise measure of holding them in a military wall, allowing them time to quiet down and listen to the assurances of such men as Young Man-Afraid-of-His-Horses, Rocky Bear, No Neck, and other progressive Indians, relieves the situation, so that, unless some accident happens, the military end of the active warfare seems a complete, final, and brilliant success, as creditable to Gen. Miles' reputation as it is to the humane and just side of his character.

"Neither should praise be withheld from Gens. Brooke, Carr, Wheaton, Henry, Forsyth, and the other officers, and men of the gallant little army, who stood much privation. In every instance when I have heard them speak they have expressed great sympathy for their unhappy foe, and regrets for his impoverished and desperate condition. They and the thoughtful people here are now thinking about the future. In fact, the Government and nation are confronted by a problem of great importance as regards remedying the existing evils.

"The larger portion of the Ogallalla Sioux have acted nobly in this affair, especially up to the time of the stampede. The Wassaohas and Brules have laid waste the reservation of the Ogallallas, killed their cattle, shot their horses, pillaged their houses, burned their ranches; in fact, poor as the Ogallallas were before, the Brules have left them nothing but the bare ground, a white sheet instead of a blanket, with winter at hand and the little accumulations of thirteen years swept away. This much, as well as race and tribal dissensions and personal enmity, have they incurred for standing by the Government. These people need as much sympathy and immediate assistance as any section of country when great calamities arouse the sympathy of the philanthropist and the Government. This is now the part of the situation that to me seems the most remarkable. Intelligent and quick legislation can now do more than the bullet.—COL. WILLIAM F. CODY ('BUFFALO BILL')"

MILITARY REPRESENTATIVES.

The Messrs. Cody and Salsbury, in collecting various groups for their Congress of Rough Riders of the World, have arranged for recognized representative soldiers of the various nations of Europe, and to this end have to-day assembled in the arena a detachment of the First Garde-Uhlan Regiment of His Majesty William II., German Emperor. They are popularly known throughout Europe as the "Potsdamer Reds." England's army will be represented by a group of 12th Lancers ("Prince of Wales Own,") and France presents a detachment of Chasseurs à Cheval. These detachments are commanded respectively by Lieutenant von Richter, Sergeant-Major Mayfield, and Lieutenant Alexandre Bayard. They will present the various evolutions and exercises of their armies, and in due course will introduce on horseback tent-pegging, lemon-cutting, Turks-Head and sabre and lance exercises.

The interest in this friendly meeting of representative cavalrymen will be added to by the presence of a detachment of our own National Soldiers (from the celebrated 6th U. S. Cavalry), who will act in consonance with the Director's idea to present an amicable study of the various military schools. These Veterans of the Plains will enable our public to more fitly comprehend the training and ability of the little American Army—that is the nucleus of the cohorts that would assemble in time of danger to the Republic—practically an army in which three-fourths of the privates would be able to do honor to shoulder straps in an emergency. The Arabs are the genuine Bedouin Soldiers of the Desert, that song, story and history have for ages celebrated, and their skill the writer will leave to the judgement of the auditor, as space prevents justice to this feature of our exhibition.

State of Nebraska

Executive Department

General W.F.Cody.

Lincoln January 6th 1891.

Rushville. Nebraska.

My Dear General.

As you are a member of my Staff, I have detailed you for special service; the particular nature of which, was made known dur-ing our conversation.

You will proceed to the scene of the Indian troubles, and communi-cate with General Miles.

You will in addition to the special service refered to, please visit the different towns, if time permit, along the line of the Elkhorn Rail-Road, and use your influence to quiet excitement and remove appre-hensions upon the part of the people.

Pleaso call upon General Colby, and give him your views as to the probability of the Indians breaking through the cordon of regular troo-ps; your superior knowlodge of Indian character and mode of warfare, may enable you to make suggestions of importance.

All Officers and members of the State Troops, and all others, will, please extend to you every courtesy.

In testimony whereof.

John M. Thayer,
Governor.

HEADQUARTERS DIVISION OF THE MISSOURI.

CHICAGO, ILLINOIS

In the Field, Pine Ridge, S.D., January 11, 1891

Brig. General W. F. Cody,

Nebraska National Guard, Present.

Sir:-

I am glad to inform you that the entire body of Indians are now camped near here (within a mile and a half). They show every disposition to comply with the orders of the authorities. Nothing but an accident can prevent peace being re-established, and it will be our ambition to make it of a permenent character. I feel that the State troops can now be withdrawn with safety, and desire through you to express to them my thanks for the confidence they have given your people in their isolated homes.

Like information has this day been given General Colby.

Very respectfully yours,

Nelson A. Miles

Major General Commanding

COSSACKS WITH THE WILD WEST.

In pursuance of their intention to assemble together, at the World's Fair, a congress of the representative horsemen of the world, MESSRS. CODY and SALSBURY have had their agents in all parts of the earth, looking for rough riders who could compete with or excel the original riders of the Wild West, the native product of America. In the Russian Cossack they found a horseman whose style was new, novel and striking, and one who could compete with the finest in the world.

These Cossacks, in the picturesque garb of the Caucasus, form the latest acquisition of the Wild West. They are a troop of "Cossacks of the Caucasian Line," under the command of Prince Ivan Makharadze.

COSSACKS FROM THE CAUCASUS.

The Prince and his comrades, it is interesting to the public to know, belong to the same branch of the great Cossack family, the Zaporogians, immortalized by Byron's "Mazeppa." Mazeppa was the hetman or chief, of the Zaporogian community of the Cossacks of the Ukraine. When Byron's famous hero came to grief at the battle of Poltava, the Cossacks fled to the Crimea, then Turkish territory, to avoid the vengeance of Peter the Great. Subsequently they were deported to the Kuban, and settled along the river as military colonists, to defend the Russian frontier against the marauding tribes of the Caucasus.

On this dangerous frontier the qualities of horsemanship that made the name of Mazeppa and his warlike followers household words throughout the whole of Europe, became still further developed in the following generations, so that the Kuban Cossacks quickly became, in many respects, the most remarkable riders in the world.

On their lithe steppe horses, as fierce and active as themselves, they proved themselves more than worthy of their sires. During the heroic struggle of the Circassian mountaineers to maintain their independence against Russia, the sons of Mazeppa's Zaporogians were found to be the only Cossacks sufficiently skilful to cope with Schamyl's wild mountain horsemen on equal terms. The Don Cossacks were lancers, and the Circassians quickly learned to dodge within their guard, and cut them down, they being among the most expert swordsmen in the world.

But the descendants of Mazeppa's Cossacks were equally expert with the sword, and so, in the matter of arms, as of horsemanship, met the enemy on equal terms. For many years the Cossacks of the Caucasian line were engaged in perpetual border warfare with the Circassian tribes. Their fighting was a series of little cavalry combats, surprises and raids, similar to the American Indian frontier wars, the finest school for the development of military horsemanship the world has seen since the days of Saladin and Cœur-de-Lion. Graduates from this fierce, wild school of saddle and sabre, the Cossacks of the Caucasian line have long enjoyed the reputation of being the flower of that vast horde of irregular cavalry, the Cossack military colonies, that have been planted along the southern frontier of the Russian Empire, from the Crimea to the Chinese border on the Pacific.

Circassian blood plainly crops out in the Cossacks of the Buffalo Bill Wild West arena. Indeed, some of them look the Circassian, even more than the Cossack. The infusion of Circassian, Georgian and Mingrelian blood, began with stirring drama of strife and romance in the days of Schamyl. Part of the policy of Russia was the suppression of the trade in Circassian beauties for the harems of Turkey, then carried on in small Turkish vessels in the Black Sea. A Cossack coastguard service was organized for the purpose, consisting of fleets of rowboats concealed in the creeks and inlets of the Caucasian coast, whence they could pounce out on the slave ships.

The vessels usually contained from forty to fifty Circassian, Georgian and Mingrelian slave girls, lovely creatures selected for the harems of the Sultan and the wealthy Pashas of Constantinople. The slaves thus captured were given to the Cossacks of the Kuban for wives; hence the sons and daughters of Schamyl's fierce opponents are as much Circassian as Cossack. The combination is a "strain" of horsemanship that has produced startling and unique results in the form of riders capable of really marvelous feats of a kind never before seen outside of Russia. Visitors to the Wild West who have marveled at the skill of the Indians and the Cowboys with the bucking mustangs, will marvel anew at the striking performances of these descendants of the famous "Mazeppa."

SOUTH AMERICAN GAUCHOS AT THE "WILD WEST."

The latest additions to BUFFALO BILL'S "Wild West" make the sixth delegation to the "Congress of the Rough Riders of the World," which MESSRS. CODY and SALSBURY are organizing in order to present the different schools of horsemanship at the Chicago World's Fair.

Having seen the performances of the Cowboy, the Indian, the Vaquero, and lastly, of the Cossacks of the Caucasian line, our appetites are considerably whetted at the prospect of seeing how wild life on the South American Pampas contrasts with theirs.

To the student of human progress, of racial peculiarities, of national characteristics, the Gauchos are a subject of investigation as remarkable as anything modern history has to show.

The Gaucho differs in many respects from the other rough riders of the only partially civilized sections of the earth. He is the product of a peculiar scheme of existence, and of savage conditions of life, that obtain in no part of the world save on the boundless Llanos of South America.

The Gauchos are the descendants of the early Spanish colonizers of the South American wilds. The fiery Hispanolian temperament, the infusion of the native Indian blood, together with the wild lonely life on the ocean-like pampas, are the conditions responsible for the production of the Gauchos.

The civilization that the Spanish colonists took with them to the Llanos gradually became subdued by the savagery of the new situation, until their descendants, the Gauchos, were as wild and ferocious as the aborigines, the Indians. They were, forsooth, compelled to adopt in no small degree the manners and customs of these latter as a means of subsistence.

Like the North American Indian, the Cowboy, the Vaquero, the Cossack, and the Prairie Scout, now for the first time in history his companion horsemen, the Gaucho is a near approach to the mythical centaur. Like them the Gaucho spends the greater portion of his life on horseback, and is associated with the wild equines of the pampas in even a more intense degree than any of the equestrian races.

GAUCHOS FROM SOUTH AMERICA.

In no other part of the world has man been so completely dependent on the horse as on the South American plains. The pampas without horses would be, for the uses of man, as an ocean without ships or boats. Hence this Gaucho breed of centaur is the natural growth of peculiar surroundings.

As the Gauchos are reputed to be the most expert lassoers in the world, considerable interest is manifested in their arrival, not only by the public, but by the Cowboys, Indians, etc. Apart from their wild fantastic personality of dress, manner, and equipment, and their horsemanship, the Gauchos will be interesting as the first to introduce to the public the use of the "bolas," for the capturing of wild animals. This instrument of the chase has been adopted by the Gauchos from the South American Indians, who, from time immemorial used it for the capture of ostriches, guanacos, and other big game.

The "bolas" consists of a number of rawhide thongs fastened to a central thong, and with an iron ball at each of the ends. The Gaucho can hurl this at a flying horse, cow, or ostrich, from a distance of sixty feet, and, causing it to inextricably entangle about the legs, bring the victim helplessly to the ground. This therefore, rather than the lasso, is his favorite weapon for the chase or fighting in war.

When the Dictator Rosas many years ago conquered Buenos Ayres, his success was largely due to the terror inspired by the reputation of his horde of Gauchos and Pampa Indians.

It may be interesting to state that from their primitive mode of existence, the Gaucho makes nearly everything connected with his "outfit," even the rude saddle from raw hide, the lasso, the "bolas," and even his boots—which are made from the skin (taken from the knee down, and shaped to the leg and foot while warm) of a freshly killed colt, sewed at the toe, thus forming practically a leather stocking without heel or sole. They are fond of music, are good dancers, retaining in many respects the poetic traditions and tendencies of their Castilian ancestors.

Enough has been said here however, of their peculiarities. They will prove a welcome acquisition to the "Wild West," for they, no less than the Cossacks, have a distinct role of their own to play in this truly gigantic enterprise of a "Congress of the World's Rough Riders."

FROM ENGLAND TO DAKOTA, THE RIO GRANDE, AMERICA, TO THE CONTINENT OF EUROPE AND RETURN OF "BUFFALO BILL'S WILD WEST" TO GREAT BRITAIN.

Since the visit of "BUFFALO BILL'S" Wild West to England and its remarkable engagement in London, at West Brompton, in 1887, a history and tour have been made, such as no organization of its magnitude and requirements ever accomplished.

A slight reference to this will be instructive and interesting, and the practical mind can,

JUBILEE YEAR, 1887, EARL'S COURT, LONDON. FAREWELL, 1892.

partially, at a glance, recognize the difficulties and arduous duties involved in its completion. A volume would be more fitting to relate its travels, its trials, and triumphant experiences. After the production in an especially erected mammoth building at Manchester, of an allegorical, pantomimic

"BUFFALO BILL" AND THE FIRST AMERICAN INDIANS THAT HAVE VISITED VENICE

and scenic representation of the history of American settlement, a return to the United States was made in a chartered steamship, *Persian Monarch*, of 6,000 tons' burden. The arrival of this vessel, outside of the company's reception, was an event of future commercial importance to the port of New York, from the fact of her being the first passenger ship of her size, draught, and class to effect a landing (at Bechtel's Wharf) directly on the shores of Staten Island, thus demonstrating the marine value of some ten miles of seashore of what in a few short years must be a part of the Greater New York.

After a successful summer season at Erastina, S. I., and New York (originating there, at Madison Square Garden, a now much copied style of Leviathan spectacle) twice crossing the Atlantic, visiting respectively Philadelphia, Baltimore, and Washington—an uninterrupted *season* of 2 years and 7 months, starting at St. Louis, Mo., on the Mississippi River, was finished in conjunction with the successful Richmond Exposition on the James River (Virginia).

The members of the organization returned over the vast continent to their respective localities (ranging from *Texan Cowboy* and *Vaquero* and his southern valley of the Rio Grande, to the

ST. PETER'S AND VATICAN, ROME.

Sioux warrior and his weather beaten foothills of Dakota), to be reunited in the following spring on board s. s. *Persian Monarch*, bound once more across the Atlantic to Havre, and consigned to the Great Universal Exhibition at Paris.

Sufficiently large grounds were secured from thirty-two different small tenants, at a great expense—two streets being officially authorized to be closed by the municipality so as to condense the whole—in Neuilly (close by the Porte des Ternes, the Bois de Boulogne, and within sight of the Exposition). Expensive improvements were made, grand stand, scenery, a $25,000 electric plant erected, and a beautiful camping ground built.

The opening occurred before an audience said to have equaled any known in the record of *Premieres* of that brilliant Capitale des Deux Mondes. President Carnot and wife, the Members of his Cabinet and families, two American Ministers, Hon. Whitelaw Reid, Hon. Louis MacLean, the Diplomatic Corps, Officers of the United States Marines, etc., etc.—a representative audience, in fact, of ladies and gentlemen of distinction, known the world over, in society, literature, art, professions and commerce, honored the Inauguration by their presence, and launched, amidst great enthusiasm, a seven months' engagement of such pronounced success as to place the Wild West second only in public interest apparently to the great Exhibition itself.

After a short tour in the South of France in the fall, a vessel was chartered at Marseilles, the Mediterranean crossed to Barcelona—landing the first band of American Indians, with accompanying associates, scouts, cow-boys, Mexican horses of Spanish descent, and wild buffaloes, etc., on the very spot where on his return to Spain landed the world's greatest explorer, Christopher Columbus. Here the patrons were demonstratively eulogistic, the exhibition seeming to delight them greatly, savoring as it did of an addenda to their national history, recalling, after a lapse of 400 years, the resplendent glories of Spanish conquests under Ferdinand and Isabella, of the sainted hero, Cristobal Colon—1492, Columbus in America—1890, "BUFFALO BILL" and the native American Indian in Spain!

Recrossing the Mediterranean, via Corsica and Sardinia (encountering a tremendous storm), Naples (the placid waters of whose noble bay gave a welcome refuge) was reached, and in the shadow of "Old Vesuvius," which in fact formed a superbly grand scenic background, another peg in history was pinned by the visit of the cow-boy and Indian to the various noted localities that here abound; the ruins of Herculaneum, Pompeii, and the great crater of "the burning mountain," striking wonder and awe as well as giving geological and geographical knowledge to the stoical "Red man."

Then the "famed of the famous cities" of the world, Rome, was next visited, to be conquered through the gentle power of intellectual interest in, and the reciprocal pleasure exchanged by, its unusual visitors, the honor being given to "the outfit" as an organization, of attending a dazzling fete given in the Vatican by His Holiness Pope Leo XIII and of receiving the exalted Pontiff's blessing. The grandeur of the spectacle, the heavenly music, the entrancing singing, and impressive adjuncts, produced a most profound impression on the astonished children of the Prairie. The Wild West in the Vatican!!

The company were photographed in the Colosseum, which stately ruin seemed to silently and solemnly regret that its famed ancient arena was too small for this modern exhibition of the mimic struggle between that civilization (born and emanating from 'neath its very walls) and a primitive people who were ne'er dreamed of in a Rome's world-conquering creators' wildest flights of vivid imaginings.

Strolling through its arena, gazing at its lions' dens, or lolling lazily on its convenient ruins, hearing its interpreted history—of Romulus, of Cæsar, of Nero—roamed this band of Wild West Sioux (a people whose history in barbaric deeds equals, if not excels, the ancient Romans), now hand in hand in peace and firmly cemented friendship with the American frontiersmen—once

COLOSSEUM, ROME.

gladiatorial antagonists on the Western Plains. They, listening to the tale on the spot, of those whose "Morituri te Salutant" was the short prelude to a savage death, formed a novel picture in historic frame! The Wild West in the Colosseum!!!

[illegible] Florence, practical Bologna, grand and stately Milan, and unique Verona were next added to the list. Verona's superb and well preserved "Arena," excelling in superficial area the Colosseum and holding 45,000 people, was specially granted for the Wild West's use; and the home of Shakespeare's love-lorn heroine placed another picture in the Red man's tour of the native land of his discoverer. The Indians were taken by "BUFFALO BILL" to picturesque Venice, and there shown the marvelous results of the ancient white man's energy and artistic architectural skill. They were immortalized by the Camera in the Ducal Palace, St. Marc's Piazza, and in the strange street vehicle of the Adriatic's erstwhile pride—the gondola—contributing another interesting object lesson to the distant juvenile student members of their tribe—to testify more fully to their puzzled senses, the fact of strange sights and marvels whose existence is to be learned of in the breadth of knowledge necessitated by their future existence.

Moving via Innsbruck through the beautifully scenic Tyrol—the Bavarian capital, Munich, with its naturally artistic instincts, gave a grand reception to the beginning of a marvelously successful tour through German-land, which included Vienna (with an excursion on the "Blue Danube"), Berlin, Dresden, Leipsic, Magdeburg, Hanover, Brunswick, Hamburg, Bremen, Dusseldorf Cologne, along the Rhine past Bonn, Coblentz, "Fair Bingen on the Rhine" to Frankfurt, Stuttgart, and Strasburg. These historic cities—with all their wealth of legendary interest, art galleries, scientific conservatories, educative edifices, cathedrals, modern palaces, ancient ruins, army manœuvrings, fortifications, commercial and varied manufacturing and agricultural industries, and the social, genial, friendly, quiet customs of its peoples—should form good instruction to the

ARENA, VERONA.

rugged rovers of the American plains—heirs to an empire as much more vast in extent and resources, as is the brightness of the diamond, after the skill expended by the lapidary, in dazzling brilliancy to the rude unpolished stone before man's *industry* lends value to its existence.

At Strasburg the management decided to close temporarily this extraordinary tour, and winter the company. Although in the proximity to points contemplated for a winter campaign (Southern France and the Rivièra), this was deemed advisable on account of the first and only attack from envious humanity that the organization had encountered. This subject will be more fully referred to in another chapter, as it necessitated the manly but expensive voluntary procedure of taking the Indians to America, to meet face to face and deny the imputations of some "ten-cent" villifiers, whom circumstances of petty political "charity," and "I-am-ism," and native buoyancy permit at times to float temporarily on the surface of a cosmopolite community, and to whose ravings a too credulous public and press give hearing.

The quaint little village of Benfield furnished an ancient nunnery, and a castle with stables and a good range; here the little community of Americans spent the winter comfortably, being feasted and feted by the inhabitants, whose esteem they gained to such an extent that their departure was marked by a general holiday, assisting hands, and such public demonstrations of regret that many a rude cowboy when once again careering o'er the pampas of Texas will rest his weary steed while memory reverts back to the pleasant days and whole-souled friendships cemented at the foot of the Vosges mountains in disputed Alsace-Lorraine.

In Alsace-Lorraine! whose anomalous position menaces the peace, not only of the two countries interested, but of the civilized world; whose situation makes it intensely—even sadly—interesting, as the theatre of that future human tragedy, for which the ear of mankind strains day and night, listening for detonations from the muzzles of the acme of invented mechanisms of destruction. The lurid-garbed angel of devastation hovers, careering through the atmos-

AFTER THE BATTLE.—FIELD OF WOUNDED KNEE—CAMPAIGN 1890–91.

phere of the seemingly doomed valley, gaily laughing, shrieking exultingly at the white-robed angel of Peace, as the latter gloomily wanders—prayerful, tearful—hopelessly hunting, ceaselessly seeking the return of modern man's boasted newly created gods: Equity, Justice, Reason!

What a field for the vaunted champions of humanity, the leaders of civilization! What a neighborhood wherein to sow the seeds of "*peace on earth and good will to all men.*" What a crucible for the universal panacea—Arbitration! What a test of the efficacy of prayer in damming up the conflicting torrents of Ambition, Cupidity, Passion, and Revenge, which threaten to color crimson the swift current of the Rhine, until its renown as the home of wealth and luxury be eclipsed by eternal notoriety as the Valley of Death!

Leaving the temporary colony under the charge of his director partner, MR. NATE SALSBURY (whose energy found occupation in attending to the details of the future), COL. CODY, the Indians, and your humble servant departed to America, arriving safely, and after refuting satisfactorily, by the Indians themselves, the base slanders that emanated in the imagination of notoriety-seeking busybodies, proceeded to the seat of the Indian difficulties in the distant State of Dakota. The splendid action of the traveled Indians, and the record of the Wild West's representatives on the spot, in the mutual interests of an excusably excited (and, to a certain extent, unintentionally wronged, yet headstrong and misguided) warlike people, and of the governmental authority, as well as of the peaceful solution of a serious situation—has been a matter of journalistic comment so recently as to need no reference here.

After a short, bloody, and mixed campaign, peace was restored, the Government authority was secured, and a selected band of Indians, composed equally of the "active friendly," headed by Chiefs "LONG WOLF," "NO NECK," "YANKTON," "CHARLEY," "BLACK HEART," and the "band of hostages" held by the military under Gen. Nelson A. Miles, at Fort Sheridan, and headed by the redoubtable "SHORT BULL," "KICKING BEAR," "LONE BULL," "SCATTER," and

"REVENGE," were given special permission to come with "BUFFALO BILL" for a short European tour, and left Philadelphia in the chartered Red Star Steamer, *Switzerland.* The significance of this fact should still forever the forked tongue of the human serpents, who without rhyme, truth, or reason, have tried to stain a fair record—which has been justly earned, and by its very prominence, perhaps, difficult to maintain.

Coming direct from the snow-capped hills and blood-stained valleys of the *Mauvaise Terre* of last winter's central point of interest, it cannot be denied that an added chapter to Indian history, and the Wild West's peculiar province of truthfully exhibiting the same, is rendered more valuable to the student of primitive man, and to the ethnologists' acquaintance with the strange people whose grand and once happy empire (plethoric in all its inhabitants needed) has been (rightfully or wrongfully) brought thoroughly and efficiently under the control of our civilization, or (possibly more candidly confessed) under the Anglo-Saxon's commercial necessities. It occurs to the writer that our boasted civilization has a wonderful adaptability to the good soils, the productive portions and the rich mineral lands of the earth, while making snail-like pace and intermittent efforts among the frigid haunts of the Esquimaux, the tangled swamps of Africa, and the bleak and dreary rocks of Patagonia.

A sentimental view is thus inspired, when long personal association has brought the better qualities of the Indian to one's notice, assisting somewhat to dispel the prejudices engendered by years of savage brutal wars (conducted with a ferocious vindictiveness foreign to our methods). The savageness of Indian warfare, born in the victim, and probably intensified by the instinctive knowledge of a despairing weakness that renders desperate the fiery spirit of expiring resistance, which latter (in another cause) might be held up for courage and tenacity as bright as that recorded in the pages dedicated to the heroes of Thermoylæ.

After all, in what land, in what race, nationality, or community can be found the vaunted vestal home of assured peace? And where is human nature so perfected that circumstances might not awaken the dormant demon of man's innate savageness?

But then again the practical view of the non-industrious use of nature's cornucopia of world-needed resources and the inevitable law of *the survival of the fittest*, must "bring the flattering unction to the soul" of those—to whom the music of light, work, and progress, is the charm, the gauge of existence's worth, and to which the listless must hearken, the indolent attend, the weak imbibe strength from—whose ranks the red man must join, and advancing with whose steps march cheerily to the tune of honest toil, industrious peace, and placid fireside prosperity.

Passing rapidly through the, to them, marvelous experience of the rail road, and its flying express train, the sight of towns, villages, cities, over valley, plain, and mountain—to the magic *floating house* (the steamer), sadly learning, while struggling with *mal de mer*, the existence of the "big waters" that tradition alone had bruited to incredulous ears, was passed the first portion of a tempestuous voyage. Its teachings were of value in bringing to the proud spirits of the self-reliant Dakotans the terrible power of nature, and of the white man's marvelous skill, industry, and ability in overcoming the dangers of the deep, the reward of patience being found in a beautifully smooth approach to land. The Scilly Islands and a non-fog encumbered journey up the English Channel—unusually bright with sunshine—the grand panorama of England's majestic shores—her passing fleet of countless examples of all kinds of marine architecture, the steaming up the River Scheldt with its dyked banks and beautifully cultivated fields, opened to the marveling nomad his first edition of Aladdin, and landed him, wonderingly surprised at the sight of thousands of white men peacefully greeting his arrival, in the busy commercial mart of Antwerp.

OFF ANTWERP

After introducing the Indians to hotel life for the first time, a tour of the city was made, among the notable points visited being the Cathedral, which grand edifice aroused their curiosity, the grand picture, Rubens' "Descent from the Cross," bringing to the minds of all—white men, 'friendlies,' and "hostiles"—the contributing cause of the late regret able campaign—the "Messiah craze"—an interest intensified by the fact that the æsthetic-looking "SHORT BULL," and some of the others, had been the leading fanatical believers (probably even apparently conscientious), promoters, and disciples of the still mysterious religious disease that lately agitated the Indian race in America. In fact, after the death of "SITTING BULL," the central figures of this strange belief were "SHORT BULL" as the religious leader, and "KICKING BEAR" as the War Chief. Grouped together with "SCATTER," "REVENGE," and others, in moody contemplation of this subject was the late defier of a mighty nation of 65,000,000 people—nearly all of whom teach or preach the truthfulness of the picture's traditions. A man in two short months transported from the indescribably desolate, almost inaccessible natural fortresses of the Bad Lands (*Mauvaise Terre*) of Dakota to the ancient city of Antwerp, gazing spell-bound on the artistic reproduction, by the renowned artist, of the red man's late dream—"The Messiah." Respect for his thoughts and the natural stoical nature of the Indian leaves to future opportunity an interesting interrogative of what passed through the mind of the subtle chief. Suffice to say that surprise at the white man's many-sided character, and the greatness of his resources in the past and present, was beginning to dawn more and more on the new tourists. Arriving the next day at Strasburg—introduction to the cowboys, the camp life, the Cathedral, the great clock, the fortifications, etc., was followed by the delight of each brave on receiving his pony, and once more with histrusty friend, the horse, theOgallalla and Brule in a fewdays felt as though "Richard was himself again."

Joining more heartily than was expected in the mimic scenes of the "Wild West," soon the ordinary routine of daily duties seemed a pleasant diversion. A grand reception in Strasburg, the tour resumed to Carlsruhe, Mannheim—including a visit to Heidelberg Castle—Mayence, Wiesbaden, to Cologne (the Rhine legends of Lurline, etc., giving interest to the Peau Rogue *en route*), Dortmund, Duisburg, Crefeld and Aix-la-Chapelle, terminated a tour of Germany filled with the most pleasant recollections. The tomb of Charlemagne (*Carolo Magno*)! The history of this great warrior was interpreted to attentive ears, a lesson being instilled by the relation that after all his glory, his battles, triumphs, and conquests in which he defeated the dusky African prototypes of the present visitors to his tomb, peace brought him to pursue knowledge, to cultivate the arts and sciences, and that after two hundred years of entombment his body was found by Otto, the Saxon, sitting erect upon a granite throne, the iron crown upon his head, imperial sceptre in right hand, while his left rested on an open volume of Holy Scriptures, the index finger pointed to the well-known passage—"What will it profit a man if he gain the whole world and lose his own soul?" Here by the grave of the founder of Christianity stood the latest novitiates to its efforts, who may yet, in following its teachings, it is hoped, make such progress through its aid and education as to furnish one of their race capable of holding the exalted chieftainship—the Presidency of their native land —the Empire of the West. Who can say—why not?

Belgium—Brussels, its Paris, brings vividly to mind, in its semblance of language, people, habits, beauty, wealth, culture and appreciation remembrances of our delightful sojourn in the capital of the how-truly-named La Belle France. Visit Waterloo. From Pine Ridge to historic Waterloo! Our immense success, courteous treatment, the repeated visits and kindly interest of that most amiable lady, the Queen, an enthusiastic horsewoman, her pleasant reference to London in the Jubilee year, combined to increase the gratitude the Wild West Voyagers feel for the treatment everywhere received in Europe since, in 1887, we invaded "Old England," and pitched our tents in the World's Metropolis—London. So, after a short season in Antwerp, our motley cargo set sail across the North Sea to make complete our farewell visit to our cousins of the isle, revel in a common language (bringing a new pleasure to the ear), hoping to receive a continuance of that amicable appreciation of our humble efforts that the past seemed to justify. Landing at Grimsby and proceeding to Leeds in Yorkshire we commenced a provincial tour of Great Britain. The reception everywhere accorded us was so hearty in its nature that a sentiment of relationship insensibly permeated the Yankee exiles. From Leeds we went to Liverpool the great shipping port, thence to Manchester where old friendships were renewed and new ones formed—a notable event being, a benefit to nineteen of the Balaclava survivors (who were indigent), resulting in great success, not only financially, but from an historic point, because of the participation in our performance of three generations, the past, present and future English soldier—in the battle scarred veterans; the Prince of Wales' Own (Lancers) and the boy cadets of the city. Sheffield with its busy factories was next visited and the Indian found a new cause for amazement in the world's cutlery city. Stoke-on-Trent with its marvelous Wedgewood ware works and other inumerable pottery industries gave another lesson in Caucasian progress and opened to the Red man new wonders in the art of table decoration. Nottingham with its busy lace looms; Leicester of historic interest and Birmingham with its mammoth iron plants in order challenged the admiration and assisted to educate the son of the forest.

Cardiff (Wales) in energy and "git up" is quite an American city, having increased in population and wealth 55 per cent. in nine years, remains on our ledger as a banner six days' stand, the receipts exceeding £10,000 ($50,000), the R. R. stocks rising on the market and one restaurant alone feeding 15,000 extra dinners to the visiting Welshmen. To Bristol the famous West of England seaport and thence to Portsmouth-Devonport the great naval-military-commercial twin cities, combined to render our visit to the South of England profitable and enjoyable. Brighton with its beauty in repose and its terror in a cyclone will long be remembered as our last stop before going to Glasgow (Scotland) where the winter was spent in a specially arranged building. Here we were made acquainted with the many sturdy virtues of the Scot, where 6,000 orphan children, impromptu sang "Yankee Doodle" on the appearance of the starry flag, will ever be remembered for the many public and social courtesies extended.

A return to the scene of our London triumphs brought a renewal of all that was pleasant and agreeable in our former experience, and brought our visit to the Old World to a close with a bright compliment under the circumstances of a Royal request to exhibit before her Most Gracious Majesty the Queen of England and Empress of India; who was thus the first and only potentate on earth to view as yet the Wild West in conjunction with the Rough Riders of the World. This episode has been so lately exploited in the press as to preclude more extended comment.

J. M. BURKE.

Leaving England with genuine expressions of regret from thousands who witnessed our departure, we now cast our fortunes, in presenting the Wild West and its Coadjutor Congress of Primitive Horseman in the metropolis of the West—without the Wild. Now comes but one regret, the absence of ability to fittingly express the deep sense of obligation we feel to every nation—every city—visited, for the kindness of each and all of every rank, every station, press, public, and officials, for the helping hands, fraternal interest, courteous treatment, and general appreciation shown us and our country's flag; so that, in returning home, we feel bound in duty to record the same, believing that, in presenting our rough pictures of a "history almost passed away," we may have done some moiety of good in simplifying the work of the historian, the romancer, the painter, and the student of the future, and in exemplifying in ourselves and experiences the fact that travel is the best educator, and that association and acquaintanceship dispel prejudice, create breadth of thought, and enhance appreciation of the truism that "one touch of nature makes the whole world kin."

SIOUX ON THE WAR-PATH: STRONGHOLD IN THE BAD LANDS OF THE HOSTILE INDIANS, CHIEFS, "SHORT BULL" AND "KICKING BEAR."

The Camp is placed upon a plateau one hundred and fifty feet above the surrounding valleys: there is only one place where men can enter it, and that place but twenty feet wide.—From the "ILLUSTRATED AMERICAN," January 10th, 1891.

www.ingramcontent.com/pod-product-compliance
Lightning Source LLC
Chambersburg PA
CBHW022017080426
42733CB00007B/632
* 9 7 8 3 3 3 7 7 2 8 0 1 4 *